SELECTED POEMS

SELECTED POEMS

PABLO NERUDA

Edited and Translated by
Ben Belitt

Introduction by Luis Monguió

Grove Press
New York

****

For Anne Schlabach

****

Published simultaneously in Canada
Printed in the United States of America

Library of Congress Catalog Card Number 61-11772
ISBN 0-8021-5102-7

Grove Press
841 Broadway
New York, NY 10003

99 00 01 02   35 34 33 32 31 30 29 28 27 26 25 24

Contents

Introduction
by
Luis Monguió

If one were to inquire today, among cultivated Hispano-Americans, which are the three major poets produced by their continent, I am sure they would return a single answer: Sor Juana Inés de la Cruz, in the Colonial era, Rubén Darío, of the "modernist" epoch, and Pablo Neruda, in our own time. Where more than two or three names are involved, local patriotism soon begins to operate; but on these three names, at once seminal and continental, there would be general agreement. The fact is a striking one, in that Pablo Neruda is a figure adored and maligned for reasons which have little to do with literature and very much to do with politics. It would be idle, even for those hostile to the aesthetic of the Chilean poet, to deny him a place of the highest importance in the tradition of Hispanic poetry. Even Juan Ramón Jiménez, winner of the Nobel Prize for Literature in 1956, and exemplar of a "pure" poetry theoretically at the opposite pole from Neruda's mystique of the "impure," was compelled to call him "a great poet; a great, bad poet"—bad in the sense that their concepts of poetry were incompatible, but by all objective standards, major.

Curiously enough, it is this poet, universally read, expounded, and criticized wherever the Spanish language is spoken, who remains so little known to English-speaking readers today. What, in brief, are the facts of Neruda's life, what is the nature of his poetry, and what, precisely, is his role in the long tradition of Hispanic literature?

The writer known to us as "Pablo Neruda" was born Neftalí Ricardo Reyes y Basoalto, in Parral, Chile, on July 12, 1904. His father, José del Carmen Reyes, was a railroad employee—"used to taking orders and giving them," as Neruda later recalled—who worked variously as section crew foreman and train conductor. His mother, Rosa Basoalto, died when the child was three or four years old, and his father shortly after took a second wife, the Trinidad Candia, cherished by the poet as "the tutelary angel of my childhood." The family moved south of his native Parral to Temuco—to that damp and densely forested region whose imagery recurs so obsessively in the poetry of Neruda. There the vision of a powerful and untamed nature lay open to his contemplation; there he received his early schooling and secondary education; there he read planlessly and voraciously; and there, too, he published his first verses in the local newspapers of Temuco and won his first prizes in the provincial "Juegos Florales."

At sixteen, Neruda went to the capital city of Santiago to continue his studies at the Instituto Pedagógico. He had no sooner arrived, than his *Canción de la fiesta (Fiesta Song)* was awarded first prize for poetry in the Spring Festival by the Students' Federation, which also published the poem in 1921. Though he remained in Santiago for some years thereafter living the life of the "literary" student-bohemian, indolence can hardly be imputed to a poet who produced five volumes of verse and prose-poetry between 1923 and 1926, as well as other pieces published at a subsequent date.

With the appearance of *Veinte poemas de amor y una canción desesperada (Twenty Love Poems and A Desperate Song*, 1924), Neruda was acknowledged as one of Chile's most promising younger poets; and the Chilean government, following a tradition of long standing, promptly sent him abroad on consular missions, as a kind of ward of Maecenas. Neruda left Chile in 1927, proceeded to Europe, traveled in the Orient, where, between 1927 and 1932, he lived successively in Rangoon, Colombo, Singapore, and Batavia, and visited adjacent areas of Asia and Oceania.

On his return to Chile in 1933, Neruda was assigned first to Buenos Aires and then to Madrid in 1934, where he was received with admiration and acclaim by a dazzling generation of Spanish poets: Federico García Lorca, Rafael Alberti, Luis Cernuda, Miguel Hernández, Manuel Altolaguirre. At their invitation he published and edited jointly the review *Caballo verde para la poesía* (*The Green Horse for Poetry*). In Madrid, too, his first and second *Residencias* first appeared together, with enormous success, in 1935. When the Civil War broke out in Spain in 1936, Neruda, heedless of diplomatic protocol, made no secret of his anti-Fascist convictions. For this reason, he was recalled to his country by the Chilean government in 1937; but a new President soon sent him off to Europe to expedite the emigration to America of Republican Spanish refugees. From 1939 to 1943, he served as Chilean consul to Mexico. The years 1935-1945 are years of progressive politicalization for Neruda, and the period of his third *Residencia*, published in 1947.

In 1943, Neruda returned to Santiago. He entered actively into politics, was elected to the Senate, and enrolled in the Communist Party of Chile. In 1948 and 1949, the conflict between the Party and the government of the Republic of Chile reached its most acute stage, and Communism was declared illegal by an act of Congress. Expelled from his senatorial post, Neruda traveled secretly through Chile and at length made his way across the border. There follow years of exile in Mexico—where, in 1950, he first published his *Canto general* (*General Song*); in Italy and France; in the Soviet Union and Red China; and then back again to Europe. In 1953, he returned to Chile, and in the same year was awarded the Stalin Prize. From that time up to the present, Neruda has continued his literary activity on Isla Negra, turning out volume after volume, with occasional intervals of travel abroad.

Luis Monguió / 9

2

The first two decades of our century—roughly, a span of twenty years from the birth of Pablo Neruda to his emergence as a poet of manifest talent—correspond to the period of maximum prestige and the subsequent decline of what historians of Hispano-American literature designate as "modernismo" (modernism). As a movement in the literature of the Spanish tongue, and of Spanish poetry in particular, the landmarks of modernism conventionally fall between the publication in 1888 of Rubén Darío's *Azul* (*Azure*), and the death of the Nicaraguan poet in 1916. An offspring of literary libertarianism, modernism was born in the restlessness and fatigue of an epoch marked by a wholesale abandonment to a vulgarized romanticism. To all that was slovenly and gross in the romanticism of its time, it opposed an insistence on delicate and taxing techniques, inspired in part by the art of the French Parnassians and symbolists, and in part by the cultivated tradition of Spanish literature itself—a return to the elegance of the medieval *mester de clerecía*, the *cancioneros* of the fifteenth century, to Góngora and the seventeenth-century baroque, and Gustavo Adolfo Bécquer in the nineteenth century. To the bourgeois cast of a tasteless romanticism, modernism held up the concept of an idealized and universalized art, patrician in character, a *fin de siècle* pursuit of art for its own sake. At its heart was the passion for noble cultural models and the Graeco-Latin world view in particular (a little colored by French translation!).

Led by Darío, the modernist poets distinguished themselves by the cosmopolitan character of their literary culture and their technical perfection—verbal, metrical, and imagistic. Their intellectual and prosodic refinement, raised to an extreme of individual expression, reflected a fastidious sensibility and a proud subjectivism: an impulse toward the exotic, the precious, the idealized, and the artificial, and a flight from the realities of nineteenth-century American positivism.

Thus modernism, like Parnassianism and symbolism, came to cultivate the rare and exquisite: Japan and the Aegean Isles, the pavilions of Versailles and the pagodas of the Orient, rococo marquises and geisha girls, libidinous abbés and samurai, Mimi Pinson and Salome—all adorned and removed from the crassness of the everyday world, or idealized as a world in itself wherein might be imagined a quest for the meaning of Flesh and Desire, the Unknown and the Fatal, the ultimate purposes of Life and Mortality—but above all, Beauty, inviolate and entire.

None the less, almost to the year of Neruda's birth, a shift was already at work in the momentum of modernism. In 1905 Rubén Darío published his *Cantos de vida y esperanza* (*Songs of Hope and Life*), in which the poet, with no loss of the cerebral and formal nuance that are the triumph of his personal style, achieved an immediate penetration of the realities of the American world. It was Darío who joined the Castilian with the Catholic, the Indian tradition with the Hispanic, and, indeed the whole epic heritage of the Conquistadors and the Liberators, as elements consubstantial with Hispano-American Beauty and Life. Suddenly, with the Cuban war of 1898 and the adventure of Panama of 1903, Darío came to feel the menace of the advancing power from the North—English-speaking, Protestant, and utilitarian. "Are we so many millions, then, speaking English?" he asked. "Shall we be silent now, the better to weep later?" In the name of an America "vital with light and with fire, with perfume and love / the great Moctezuma's America and the Inca's / the fragrant America of Christopher Columbus / America, Catholic and Spanish," and in behalf of a culture seeking union "in spirit, in language, and passion," he returned an intransigent "No!" It is this aspect of modernism that historians have underscored with the unwieldy epithet of *mundonovismo* (New Worldism), or The Return to America.

Close on the heels of these developments, the disaster of World War I—a war which was to compel so many Americans and non-Americans to question the basis of the cultural leadership of a Paris or a Berlin hitherto accepted without question—began to undermine the modernist structure. The intellectual crisis, a by-product of the war, shattered the sovereign fiction of an archetypal culture—of *the* culture, intact in itself, predicated by modernism. At the same time, in all that pertained to form, the reiteration of stereotypes and styles between the years 1880-1920, was steadily depleting its force.

In Europe, the philosophical and literary crisis was reflected in movements such as cubism, futurism, Dadaism, ultraism, creationism, and finally, in 1924, the surrealist explosion, with its double assault on prewar literature and the rational. In the realm of poetry these movements revolted against symbolism and decadence, the European parallels of Hispano-American modernism.

At this moment of crisis for the literature of the world, Pablo Neruda arrived in Santiago de Chile in 1920.

3

The Neruda of 1920 is a Neruda fired by a vision of the natural world of South Chile which never abandoned him. It was his way, even as a child, to observe: "I'm going out hunting poems"; and in later years he was to recall:

> What I saw first were
> trees and ravines,
> all that blazon of flowers, a splendor gone barbarous,
> humid perspectives where forests were holocausts

and winter rampant on the other side of a world.
My childhood is made of wet shoe-leather, a wreckage
of tree-trunks brought down in the forest, devoured
by lianas and beetles; mild days on the oats. . .

On the other hand, he brought with him to Santiago the whole ferment of his indiscriminate reading: sentimental and romantic reading (Diderot, Bernardin de Saint-Pierre, Victor Hugo); tales of adventure and the faraway (Jules Verne, Emilio Salgari); psychological realism (Strindberg, Gorky); erotic realism (Felipe Trigo); and lesser modernists like Vargas Vila. The covers of those volumes, many of them translations, mass-produced for cheap consumption in the mills of Barcelona and Valencia (Sopena, Maucci, Sempere) come readily to mind; for the taste of a generation of provincial adolescents, famished for reading matter, was nourished (and sometimes debased) by them. Even the pseudonym adopted by the poet—Neruda—, it may be, follows the model of the author of the *Tales of Malá Strana*, the Czech, Jan Neruda, whose translation into the Spanish reached the public—if memory serves—in the Colección Universal of Madrid, in olive green dust jackets, a peseta a volume.

In Santiago, the young poet went on to broaden the base of his reading. His firsthand acquaintance with the staples of French poetry is obvious. Arturo Torres-Rioseco remembers a schoolteacher in Chile in his own youth who cautioned his charges, "Don't waste your time on Spanish and Chilean writers: life is short and there's so much to be read in French." Certainly there is no lack of Hispano-American testimony dating back to those years to make clear which of the French poets were most favored by South American readers: Albert Samain, a symbolist of the second order much in vogue in the Hispanic world (for his frequent allusions to Catholic ritual, perhaps, and his décor); the older pantheon of Baudelaire, Verlaine, Rimbaud, and Mallarmé. Neruda, however, appears to have given equal attention to the great Hispano-American modernists, from the tutelary Darío, to the younger generation of Julio Herrera y Reissig, and particularly, Carlos Sabat Ercasty.

It is hardly surprising, under the circumstances, that the earliest writings of Neruda, *La Canción de la Fiesta* and *Crepusculario (Twilight Book*, 1923) should be teeming with echoes. The poet himself was the first to concede it: "Distant voices mingled with mine / I'm aware of it, friends!" It is plain that his juvenile pieces are highly derivative, "modernistic" in versification, in language, and the choice of themes. They abound in alexandrine quatrains, in votive lamps and ogives, in Beloveds with a capital B, in Pelleases, Melisandes, Paolos, and Helens. But it should be equally clear to attentive readers that if his poems embody the death rattle of a movement, they also exhibit the prodromes of a personal Neruda, a Neruda who a few short years later was to discover his private inflection and his individual style.

I refer, of course, to that Neruda whose senses open directly on the reality of the world around him—not an idealized fiction of the world, but a world of quotidian substances, fair and foul by turns; a Neruda of photographic perceptiveness, standing guard with his hearing, his vision, his touch, and his nostrils—a world of real objects like the blind beggar's tambourine and the branding iron, of ashes and anvils and railroad trestles; and above all, the seeding earth, the line of a furrow, trees, beaches, and water (that omnipresent water! rain, rivers, seas, tears); open to sensual love, to his own body and the body of ungratified desire. It is in that world of sensation brought to bear by a child upon insects and birds and partridge eggs, the scarred face of a man, picture post cards, the smell of cut wood, the *copihue's* color, and the taste of slaughtered lamb's blood, that the very earliest work of the poet is distinguishable from the prevailing verse of his time. By their aid Neruda was, in effect, opening a breach in the façade of all that was precious and remote in the cerebral world of the modernist, submitting his whole being to passions that dwell in a world of real things, both noble and ignoble, in whatever guise they happened to suggest themselves to him. In his receptivity to immediate intuition, to the quotidian, the coarse, and the commonplace—to all that earlier modernists would have scorned as "unpoetical" and antipoetic—the youthful Neruda aligned himself boldly with those other Hispano-American poets of his era who confronted a world strange to their literary patrimony—with the Mexican, Ramón López Velarde of *La sangre devota* (1916), for one, and the Peruvian César Vallejo, of *Los heraldos negros* (1918); by no means poor company.

In *Veinte poemas de amor y una canción desesperada,* Neruda's deference to the metrical forms and traditional strophes of the modernists, along with other innovations then in fashion, is still apparent; but the temper and tone of his verse is no longer the characteristic temper of modernism. Even for that most sensual of modernists, Rubén Darío, the flesh was idealized, if not, indeed, divinized, beatifically concentering on the mystery of the world, to symbolize "the eternity of the probable." In *Veinte poemas,* on the other hand, the flesh remains corporeal and the body, a kind of geography which, like the geography of the natural world, has its highways and river beds, its mountains and chasms. Nothing could be more substantive than the love of *Veinte poemas,* nothing closer to animal and vegetal nature, or more germinal. In it the poet appears rooted like wheat or a vineyard or a pine, "drunk with turpentine and long kisses"; and woman is a terrestrial shell in which the earth sings. He couples woman with the earth, the phases of

Luis Monguió / 15

passion with the phases of the year; almost obsessively he matches the cycle of planting and seeding and harvest, the mutations and returns of the vegetal, the animal, and the human worlds. There is a cosmic quality to his identification of earth and humanity, which persists, like an instinct, as a powerful constant of the poetry and the intuition of Neruda. Years later, when Neruda in the *Residencias* was compelled to envision a world in displacement, the fixed points which remained were the objects grasped by his senses: his own "symmetrical stature of twinned legs," his mouth and his arms, his face, skin, teeth, and hair; woman with the "health of the furious apple"; tangible natural objects (I was about to say *edible*), like the celery, the wine, and the wood of his *Tres cantos materiales (Three Material Songs)*. Later still, in the period of *Las alturas de Macchu Picchu (The Heights of Macchu Picchu)*, there rises out of the stones themselves and the seminal lime, an "infinitesimal life winged with clay," reborn with the poet, planted by his blood and his language into the mountain ranges of America. Even his most recent *Odes* are veritable canticles of material passion to the objects of this world: artichokes, copper, fish, onions, oil. In the *Odes*, as always in Neruda, love is the "bread of the fragrance of woman," to be seized by the poet's intensities, sensuous, sensual, material.

This instinctive materialism of Neruda, this ardent surrender to an encircling universe (which goes deeper than mere New Worldism), this blind faith in the truth of the senses, erupted upon Neruda's time with the impact of a new romanticism, intuitional and primitive, a bolt aimed at the idealism and intellectualism of the modernists. *Veinte poemas*, in the realm of American poetry, suggests the relationship of the Douanier Rousseau's painting to the sophisticated tradition of impressionism, or the architecture of Gaudí to the *art nouveau*.

Shortly afterward, there appeared the briefer *Tentativa*

del hombre infinito (*Venture of Infinite Man,* 1925) to mark a further phase in the liquidation of the literary heritage of the past, and the quest for a mode of expression intrinsic to Neruda himself. In *Tentativa*, the surrender to intuition is total: in the interests of his vision, Neruda is prepared to dispense with rhyme, with consistent patterns of meter, with traditional stanzaic usage, the discursive structure of language, punctuation, and the logical formalization of meaning. He grapples directly with language itself—with the blockage that limits the immediate expression of whatever wells up from within, or is aimed at him from without; his intent is to work outwardly, from within, as well as with exterior forces brought to bear by alerted sensation on the intimate world of his being and feelings. Impulses are meshed and confused in an upsurge of seemingly disjunct images, bubbling and churning in the agony of his quest for form and expression:

> I see a bee circling now the bee is no more
> little fly of the paraffin legs while your flight strikes
>   again
> I bend my head helplessly
> I follow a strand that leads to some presence at least
>   a fixed point of sorts
> I hear silence adorning itself with a billow's successions
> vertiginous echoes revolve and return and I sing out
>   aloud.

So it is that Neruda (before his twenty-second year, incredibly enough) came to reflect at a point of his poetic development, an American aspect of the philosophical and aesthetic crises of the Western postwar world—that aftermath of World War I to which I have already alluded. If the reasoning intelligence could spawn monsters of war—for "reason produces monsters"—perhaps (so the premise ran)

Luis Monguió / 17

by freeing the psyche from the repressions of reason, a different order of reason might be found, "which reason knows not of"—a kind of liberty, if you will, a new and more human order of liberty. A presentiment of that psychical liberty (already in the air of the twenties) is apparent in this poetry that tramples the "laws" of the intellect and presses toward an understanding of objects, ideas, and emotions; not analytically, but by immediate and total apprehension of them. It is a poetry committed to the satisfaction of man's emotional needs, and not his discursive intelligence. Its medium is a literature that structures itself on emotive association, like the subconscious, and works in the flux of sensation and thought—simultaneously or by discontinuous bursts; by accumulation or short circuit; by repetitive and chaotic enumeration; or by spontaneous synthesis—a process, to all appearance arbitrary and wayward, but moved, nevertheless, by real states of being that find their justification simply by coming to be. The consequences for poetry were hermetic—a mode of expression unique to the identity of the poet, a cryptography which the reader was compelled to accept without question, sharing in the work and the substance of the poem to rebuild and remake and retrace the paths through the psyche of the writer-medium.

4

Since all moves so rapidly and memory is fleeting, it is worth bearing in mind, as a datum of history, the temper of that epoch, at once so close to our own and removed from it, before passing on to assess Neruda's accomplishments in the years 1925-1935, with which Ben Belitt begins his translations: the period of *Residencia en la tierra* I & II (*Residence on Earth*) published in 1933 and 1935, and the first poems of *Residencia* III (1947). Here all falls away; here the forms hitherto acceptable to the poet appear spurious or inadequate or used up: Euclid's geometry, Newton, the rational intelligence, the Parthenon, Christian mores, the liberal State. The old gods have perished, and in the midst of a fluid and residual world Neruda bears innocent witness:

> I weep in the midst of invasions, confusions,
> gross with my tastes, giving ear
> to a pure circulation, to a massing of matter
> yielding my footsteps to whatever befalls, undirected,
> whatever breaks forth from below, clothed with chains
> and carnations
> I dream, and endure what remains of my perishing
> being.
>
> . . . .
>
> I go lonely among scattering substances,
> rain falls, and resembles me,
> in its monstrous derangements it resembles me: even
> rain in a dead world
> goes lonely, repelled in its downfall, with no resolute
> form.

"With no resolute form"—like the watches metamorphosed into fried eggs, in the painting of Dalí. We must reckon here with a dismemberment of poetry, a disorder like that of the world in which Neruda himself moved: a world of ashes and powdery glances, of papers and brooms, pallid days, decrepit objects, graveyards and tailor shops, and orthopedic appliances. To project the anguish of such a world, Neruda gathers symbols, images, and metaphors; he seems to peer at the world through the lens of a monstrous microscope that enlarges to maximum proportions whatever is sad or despairing or topsy-turvy or absurd. What he saw, he set forth in a language grammatically anomalous, displaced by rhetorical images, in panting and strenuous rhythms, as if the expressive force to which he had yielded his faculties impelled him to eject the content of his vision without respite, respiration, or order.

If we recall that the period of the *Residencias* is also the epoch of ascendent surrealism, we can account for certain idiosyncrasies of Neruda's poetic language in these terms. It was the boast of surrealists to have grasped the reality of a certain process of mental and affective association hitherto ignored; to affirm a disinterested and untrammeled play of thought and the omnipotence of the dream. By the aid of psychic automatism, their hope was to touch the very function of thinking itself, disengaged from the controls of reason and aesthetic and moral preoccupations. Thus, in the free association of images, in the bold use of psychic and verbal relations apparently disjunct and gratuitous, in automatism, autohypnotic verbalization, hallucination, and the dream work of so many of the poems in *Residencia* I & II, Neruda seems to employ familiar surrealist procedures. Yet over and above his assault on the impasse of subconscious and rational intelligence or the quest for a new and absolute order of reality—"surreality"—Neruda in his *Residencias* remains fundamentally the intuitional materialist already abundantly discussed. For this reason, matter, for Neruda, remains "nuptial"; for this reason the poet, in a disintegrating world to which he bears such exact witness, seeks salvation not in surrealist metaphysics, but the plenum of physical things.

If classical geometry will not serve, for example, there is always the celery stalk, from which "linear lightnings break clear"; if the Parthenon sags, the celery stalk has its "doves with a volute's propensities"; if society totters, "crisp energies" burst from the wellsprings of nature itself in "a river of life, indispensable threads," to pierce the physical being and "make known what is dark in the brightness, the rose of creation." For this reason, too, at those crises of tension when all waits in the balance and the poet, face to face with dissolving reality ("Brussels," *Residencia* III) declares himself "vegetal, lonely," the reader remains undismayed. He is aware that, for Neruda, nature and matter, the whole of the vegetal universe, presage life and well-being, and not death and extinction; nor does he find it an occasion for surprise when Neruda, a few pages later, reveals himself "born in the forests" again:

Again
I hear, like the fire in the smoke,
the approach of a birth blazing out of terrestrial cinder,
light crowded with petals,
and dividing the earth
in a river of wheat the sun touches my mouth again
like a long-buried tear become seed.

During these same years, Neruda was coming to sense the inadequacy of irrational philosophy and his own literary preconceptions. For surely the instinctual forces freed from the repressions of an imperfect reason and a no less imperfect society by the irrational, may be true and benign, or bestial and evil. Who, of his generation, or who of a subsequent generation, with a smattering of history, needs to be advised of the consequences of the wholesale unleashing of the instincts? Certainly Neruda, an unimpeachable witness, was well aware of them. In *Las furias y las penas* (*The Woes and the Furies*, 1939) he noted provisionally: "The world has changed and so has my poetry." Clinging fast to the earth and the body and matter in the first two *Residencias*, Neruda survived the derangement, disintegration, loneliness, and non-being that ambushed and plundered a world and rose to another life, another being—still clinging to earth and to body and matter.

Luis Monguió / 21

5

What was it that altered the personal life of Neruda at this time? Between 1936 and 1939, the Spanish Civil War exploded upon the world of his race and his language, and the routines of his life in Madrid, wrenching fibers of experience hitherto untouched, and probing behind the world of material things to the material basis of human fraternity:

> I among men bear the same wounded hand,
> suffer the same reddened cup
> and live an identical rage.

Neruda suddenly saw himself no longer estranged, but "reunited"—not with accidents of matter, in blind processes of cosmic fatality, as before, but with men, in processes of will. Previously it was his instincts that enabled him to "endure what remains of my perishing being"; now his will made powerful demands upon him. Moving out of the shadow of the past, Neruda offered to the world a changed heart, a new source of perception firmly aligned with suffering and embattled mankind.

Years before, in 1922, another Hispano-American poet— the Peruvian, César Vallejo—published a volume of verse (*Trilce*) similar in idiom and feeling to *Tentativa* and *Residencia* and spoke mordantly of the grief and bereavement of life in a world gone absurd. From that time to the present he had kept silent; then, in *España, aparta de mí este cáliz* (*Spain, Remove From Me This Cup*) and *Poemas humanos*, both written between 1936 and 1938, the trauma of war touched the springs of poetic creation. Here, "heart-bound to his skeleton," a compassionate Vallejo enters the suffering world in behalf of that:

presence beside me
from whose neck there enormously rises and falls
unsustained by the length of a thread and untaught,
all my hope.

The "hope" of Vallejo was man's hope—all those he acknowledged as brothers, and with whom Neruda also took common cause—for whom Neruda now sang. For Neruda in *España en el corazón* (*Spain in the Heart*, 1937) makes clear his "demand for a song / with explosions, the desire / for gargantuan song," for a "dazzle of hopes." It is an act of creative will, a commitment later to take the form of a "song" that may well be called "gargantuan": the *Canto general* of 1950.

The most obvious difference between the Neruda of the *Residencias* of 1933 and 1935, and the *Canto general* and the works that follow, *Odas elementales* (*Elemental Odes*, 1954), its sequels, *Nuevas odas elementales* (*New Elemental Odes*, 1956), *Tercer libro de las odas* (*Third Book of Odes*, 1957), *Estravagario* (*Book of Vagaries*, 1958), *Navegaciones y regresos* (*Voyages and Homecomings*, 1959)—not to mention his volumes of political verse like *Las uvas y el viento* (*The Grapes and the Wind*, 1954)—is his palpable choice of a style. Previously, Neruda had declared himself a poet at the service of immediate experience, striving to encompass with a stroke the whole ferment of his sensibility. In that expressive exertion, that agonized struggle of being and feeling and articulating, he did not hesitate to sacrifice intelligibility. Now he sought above all things to communicate—to abandon whatever might tax the understanding of his reader. The poetry of this period, with the exception of minor idiosyncrasies of typography, is readily reducible to conventional operations of meaning; and the language is lucid. In his newly found fellowship with mankind, the very humblest, Neruda's wish is to understand and be understood by all. Now:

> I don't write to be imprisoned by other books
> or the lily's incarnate apprentices
> but for simple sojourners whose need
> is the moon and the water, the immutable bases of
>   order,
> bread, wine, and schoolhouses, guitars and the tools
>   of their trade.

He would have his poems:

> useful and usable
> like metal and cereal
> that waits for the plowshare
> tools for the hand.

He would be simple:

> Simplicity,
> be with me, assist in my birth,
> teach me again how to sing
> a floodtide of virtue and truth,
> a crystalline victory.

His wish is not so much to *approach* a people, as to *be* them:

> Each day I learn something,
> combing my hair every day
> I think what you think,
> walk
> as you walk,
> and eat as you do,
> I circle my love with my arms
> as you circle yours,
> and then

when all's known
and each is made equal,
I write
I write with your life and my own.

This emphasis upon poetry as communication, as social action, reflects a collectivism preached two centuries before by Herder. The notion of poetry as "useful and usable" labor, as a "tool" of the "true and the virtuous," brings to mind the millenial vision of Horace's *Ars Poetica*, neoclassical concepts of poetry as a public utility, and the American romantics of the first decades of the Independence. An ethical temper of poetry, of art as action and philosophy as action, characterizes a whole trend of Hispanic tradition— Quevedo, Jovellanos, Bello, Unamuno, Antonio Machado— that returns in Neruda by the force of its own historic momentum. Neruda also would impose certain limits and obligations on poetry; he would also subject his art to a discipline of reason and will, of order and intelligence. The degree to which he has achieved his purposes without sacrificing his lyricism is today a matter of fashionable debate among Hispanic critics—a quarrel in which political sympathies and antipathies often play a more important role than literature, and in which sweeping judgments of the total stature of the recent work of the Chilean poet are too frequently based on fragments of his *oeuvre*. All things abound in the Vineyard of the Master; and in the latter books of Neruda it is possible to gather the grapes or the dry sticks, according to the taste of each critic.

No one will deny that on many occasions the verse of Neruda is closer to political reportage and homily than to poetry: "I fixed up some food for the kids and I left. / I wanted to get to my husband in Lota. / As anyone can tell you, the local militia was out; / no one could move without permit / and they didn't much go for my looks. There were orders / from González Videla, before he went in to spout off his fine speeches / and that had the rest of us scared." Nevertheless, it would be hard to deny that in most of these poems, the circumstantial detail, the politics, the propaganda, the truth, the bias, the anger, the hate (call it what you please) have in no way impaired his poetic intensity. To be sure of that one has only to read, in Mr. Belitt's translations, poems like "The Beggars," "Sleeping Assassin," "The Dictators," "Hunger in the South," "Cristóbal Miranda," and "Toward Mineral."

It is precisely this deceptive simplicity, in assessing *Canto general*, that invites dangerous oversimplification. The obsession with the political position of Neruda, or, if I may be permitted such a word, the *politicism* that permeates the whole of Hispano-American life, has diminished the scope of *Canto general* for many readers to the topical and the political. For indeed, both are present. America, for Pablo Neruda, is a perpetual battleground for the forces of men joined and committed in love to their land, and the forces of violent men seeking to rape and possess it. On one hand is the soil of the continent itself, before names were devised for it, with its natural riches, its fertility, and its prototypal people augmented in the course of time by men of all races who felt, or have come to feel, a flame of freedom and charity in their hearts, from Fray Bartolomé de las Casas or Alonso de Ercilla, to San Martín, Lincoln, and Martí to the striker jailed in Iquique or an *ejidatario* from Sonora: all Americans. On the other hand, there are rapacious and covetous men, from Columbus to Cortés, to Rosas and García Moreno, to a Somoza or a Trujillo and the masters of Anaconda Copper and United Fruit. The struggle between the two factions, Neruda prophesied, would be resolved in the triumph of the former over the violence of the latter. It is a commanding aspect of his vision; and given the importance of Neruda and the zeal with which he is read by many, he must be placed among the movers and shakers of a climate of opinion, or better still, a spiritual stance, or revolutionary nationalist sentiment that prevails throughout all Latin America. This is all that many, inside Hispano-America and outside it, have come to see in *Canto general,* without troubling themselves to probe deeper. This viewpoint is a betrayal of a work of art; for one need not be a sibyl to discover more, ever so much more, in it.

Canto general is a work to be read as a cosmogony, a Nerudian vision of the origin and creation of the world and American man. As teleology or as vision, Neruda has wrought as he must, pursuing the course of creation, reality, and life that is proper and possible to love. If there is a fixed point in Neruda, from his childhood up to the present, it is his immersion of his being in his land, his fatherland, his instinctual materialism. In *Canto general* it is water and earth, the air and the primordial slime, self-spawned and begetting the beasts, vegetation, and men of America, that he celebrates, above all.

For the content of Nerudian song is life and victory over personal death: altruistically. Reborn in himself, his renascence takes new hold of matriarchal matter itself. He is son of that mother; and all natural things—dust, plant, beast, man—are his brothers and mentors. In his darker moments, Neruda had asked of himself: what is man? where is abiding, indestructible life? Only the dead answered; but later, on the "heights of Macchu Picchu," in the heart and brain of maternal America, he came upon his vision. The corn kernel ascended and descended again; water flew and descended again with the snow; colored with clay, his hand left the clay and was one with the clay again; the cradle of lightning and man was the same. By love, by "infinitesimal life winged with the earth," he existed. There was one death and one life: not my life or yours, but the life of all beings and things—the crocodile's mother, the petal, the water lily, the thousand bodies blackened by rain and night whose blood flows in our veins and who speak with our voices. For this reason Neruda, after writing in "Yo soy" ("I am"), "Let me die now," "I make ready my death," announced with equal assurance, "I'm not ready to die. I leave now / on this day of volcanoes / for a multitude and a life." He writes:

> I leave others to mope of the charnel-house . . .
>
> The world
> has the naked hue of the apple: the rivers
> gouge out a ransom of savage medallions
> and a tender Rosalie lives everywhere
> with her playfellow, Juan . . .

Between the *Heights of Macchu Picchu* and "I Am," Neruda has packed the whole history and life of America, all the politics and myths dearest to him. In *Canto general* he interprets history according to Karl Marx, writes a new *Légende des siècles* like Victor Hugo, and prophesies like William Blake: it is one and the same. The truths he encountered were known to him instinctively as a child: "Nature there [in Temuco] went to my head like strong whisky. I was barely ten at the time, but already a poet." Drunk with nature, earth, and humanity, today, as always before:

> I have here before me only seeds,
> a sweetness, a dazzling extension.

In the four volumes of *Odes* he has continued to press for the passionate disclosure of beings and things; and the same may be said for the more technically complex *Estravagario* (1958). All his books are testimonials, all his chants are material, all his songs, love songs: love of atoms, barbed wire, lemons, moons, cats, pianos, printing presses, man, life, and poetry.

6

Neruda was born in the Chilean backwoods, in a frontiersman's world, face to face with the real, deep in nature's potency. He is a son of that New World, surging, creating, and coming to be, in quest of his personal forms and his destiny. We may readily discount what is fortuitous in the man and his poetry—modernism, surrealism, communism: what may be viewed as a succession of evangels: the gospel according to Rubén Darío, according to André Breton, according to Marx—and recover in his total achievement, even in the most hermetic of his poems, a gust from the genesis of America. It blows from the now outmoded *Crepusculario* and *Veinte poemas*, from the "sonatas and destructions" of the *Residencias*, from his *Canto general* and the most recent of his *Odes*. He has mingled, baroquely or romantically, as you will, literature and life, nature and poetry.

He was aware of this when he wrote, in *Childhood and Poetry* (1954): "We come upon poetry a step at a time, among the beings and things of this world: nothing is taken away without adding to the sum of all that exists in a blind extension of love." Montesinos has said of the old Spanish baroque that it is "the art of denying oneself nothing." It is so with Neruda, who has also denied himself nothing, faithful to the tradition of the omnivorous poets "of flesh and bone."

Berkeley, California
December, 1960

—Translated by Ben Belitt

Luis Monguió / 29

Translator's Foreword

The translator of Pablo Neruda comes to his task fore-warned by a poet hardened to the condescension of his detractors and the scruples of his well-wishers:

> I wrote down five verses:
> one green,
> one shaped like a breadloaf,
> the third like a house going up,
> the fourth one, a ring,
> the fifth one
> small as a lightning flash . . .
>
> Then came the critics: one deaf,
> and one gifted with tongues,
> and others and others:
> the blind and the hundred-eyed,
> the elegant ones
> in red pumps and carnations,
> others decently clad
> like cadavers . . .
> some coiled in the forehead
> of Marx or thrashing about in his whiskers;
> others were English,
> just English . . .
>
> (*Oda a la crítica*)

On the other hand, there have been many to remind us that the poetry of Pablo Neruda is in itself a species of translation: time and again, in exploring the *Residencias*, Amado Alonso[1] is led to invoke the analogy of the "transla-

---

[1] *Poesía y estilo de Pablo Neruda: Interpretación de una poesía hermé-tica.* Amado Alonso. Editorial Sudamericana: Buenos Aires. 1951.

tor," as if to remind us of the relativism of all linguistic transactions. "So oddly ordered are the words of this poetry," he writes, "that the phrases at times seem to be translated from a foreign language and retain something of the ordering drive of the originating language." His style is described as "oneirical," "hermetic," disintegrative, wayward, irrational, surreal, and olfactory. Among the poems "shaped like bread or a ring," and those "like a house going up," we are urged to take note of eruptive and vegetal processes, intuitional configurations, images of destruction, and "the melting away of the world." On the whole, however, the genius of Neruda is torrentially affirmative, and makes a discipline of even its excesses. The stature and fascination of his vision lie in a movement of thought keyed to its own impulses and alert to its own intrinsicality, in which the successions of the verse and the successions of intuition are one and the same, and the volume and character of the feelings and fantasy serve an organic momentum, an "ascending and descending play of intensity."

The choice of the translator, in such a case, is clear; he may rest on the completed action of the poet and compile a memorandum of *words* removed from the drives of the originating excitement; or he may press for a comparable momentum in his own tongue and induce translation accordingly. It seems to be the fate of the translator always to echo the cry of Rilke's "Ninth Elegy": "Alas, but the *other relation*! What can be carried across?" and speculate mistrustfully:

> Are we, perhaps, here just for saying: House,
> Bridge, Fountain, Gate, Jug, Olive Tree, Window—
> possibly: Pillar, Tower?

The poetry of Pablo Neruda, however, is not so easily gratified. His art leaves little room for semantic optimism, or the tactical disengagement of the translator from the shock of those "other relations" which are the primary mode of its excitement. It is "ignorant" and tentative, "oceanic" and vulnerable, precisely because it postulates the enigmatic character of the substantive and communicative world. His vision, like Whitman's, is "hankering, gross, mystical, nude," but his art shows the stresses of a more protean identity, the anguish of a more unappeasable commitment. The triumph of the *oeuvre* of Pablo Nerudo is to conclude, after two decades of doctrinal idealism in which even the onion and the soup spoon are pressed into the service of dialectic, with, *Estravagario* "a book of vagaries," and a valediction which must surely concern the translator as much as it does the reader:

> I pass on to the other side of the page
> and am never lost to your sight:
> I vault through transparency,
> a swimmer of heaven,
> and return to grow
> infinitesimal, till a day
> when the wind bears me off
> and even my name is unknown to me
> and I wake to non-being;
>
> when my singing shall sound in a silence.
>
> (Testamento de otoño)

For all his insistence on the "poetry of the impure," the "massing of things, the use and disuse of substances," the theme of the *oeuvre* repeats Rimbaud's "Je est un autre!" ("The I, is an Other"), Lorca's "Yo ya no soy yo / Y ni mi casa es ya mi casa." ("I am I now no longer / And my house is no longer my house"), and the crepuscular cry of his youth: "Nosotros, los de entonces, ya no somos los mismos."

("We, we of the lapsed world, are no longer the same.")

The whole of the *Canto general* (*General Song*) offers a striking case in point; it is, in effect, a pageant of contrasts and metamorphoses. Here, it would seem, only the primary images of creation—Deluge, Leviathan, and the displacement of men and events that goes by the name of History—will serve to evoke the shaping purposes of the poet. Signed, in the concluding lyric, "today, 5 February, in this year of 1949, in Chile, in 'Godomar de Chena,'" it towers above the achievement of Neruda with the accumulated wealth and detritus of a lifetime. It is, like *Moby Dick* and *Leaves of Grass*—whose cadences should convey it to American ears—a *progress*: a total book which enacts a total sensibility. It moves in a framework of awe as imponderable as the cosmological figures of Job, and improvises upon the central illumination of a lifetime. It ransacks the commonplace, the topical, the singular, in its search for the generic. The premise which it seems to have served is that imagination and the political factor, the meditative life and the existential datum, comprise a single reality. In its strengths and its weaknesses, it epitomizes the double mind of messianic romanticism: the passion for the infinite and the empirical, the private fable in apocalyptical guise.

One is tempted, in casting up the sum of *Canto general*, to deal in terms of extension alone; for quantitatively, the design of the work is the most extravagant that the poetry of our time has produced. For some, like Amado Alonso, it will call to mind the "frescoes of Michelangelo"; for others, the splendors of Orozco will seem the more exact analogy. It is, in the phrase of Chesterton, a specimen of the "gigantesque." It begins at the Beginning, as a god might invoke the categories of the Creation, to fashion a habitable globe out of "Vegetation," "Some Beasts," "The Birds Arrive," "The Rivers Appear," "Minerals," "Men." It moves on to principalities, forces, powers—the "spaces of spirit" through which life looks toward death, "resurrections out of nowhere," and enters the durative factor of history.

The history is, to be sure, the American Dream as the *norteamericano* has seldom been permitted to see it—the Hispanic tradition, with Cortés, Balboa, Magellan, Bolívar, Zapata, and Juárez as its demigods, the *pampas* and capitals of Mexico and South and Central America as its theater, the perfidies and restorations of Chile as its fable, and the metamorphoses of the poet—as patriot, fugitive, exile, prophet, revolutionary, somnambulist, and bard—as its drama. It concludes, in fifteen books and 568 pages, in a veritable psalter of Isaianic salutations, with a doxology of the "Fruits of the Earth," "Wine," "Great Joy," "Death," "Life," "Testaments," "Depositions," and the divinized sign of the ego: "Yo Soy": "I Am."

A just criticism of Neruda's conception, however, would have to concern itself with less sumptuous considerations, as well. For the *Canto general*, despite its multinational address, is also a *Canto general de Chile*. Like *Leaves of Grass*, it is a work inseparable from a national scene and an identifying personality. Whatever its continental sweep and bravura, it deduces both the lyrical occasion and the vision which it serves, from the *tierra* of the poet's birth. Despite his hymns to Stalingrad, his styptic denunciations of United Fruit and Coca-Cola, his early exercises in the crepuscular and erotic French "modernist" genre, his Whitmanese, Neruda remains, in the words of Torres-Rioseco,[2] "the Chilean Indian from Parral."

For the North American reader, it is true, the topical

---

[2]*New World Literature: Tradition and Revolt in Latin America*. Arturo Torres-Rioseco. University of California Press. Berkeley and Los Angeles. 1949.

exactitudes of the poet are likely to be forfeit; for this reason I have held them to a minimum in this selection. Yet it is a mark of Neruda's greatness that his poetry does not wait upon historicity to deliver the imaginative and moral splendor of his theme. He transcends both the programmatic materialism of his political stance and the histrionics of his attitude. Along the fraying margins of the "political subject," Neruda moves at will from invective and reportage—from *"porfiristas* of Mexico, 'gentlefolk' of Chile, *pitucos* of the Jockey Club of Buenos Aires, the sticky filibusterers of Uruguay, Ecuadorian coxcombs, clerical lordlings of every party"—to the incandescence of the lyrical occasion. Though he is master of the Goya-esque cartoon ("The Dictators") in which compassion bites like an etcher's corrosive, he has also Whitman's capacity for moving from dimension-in-length to dimension-in-breadth-and-depth, opening the stanza to enormous increments of detail and floating the burden of the phenomenal world on the unanswerable pathos of a mystery.

Few will deny that the tyranny of the partisan position is apparent throughout the whole of this proud and obsessional book. In the end, however, it is the *"other* relation" that constantly draws the poet away from the entrenched point and the limited commitment: from "false astrologies," political slogans, and all the apparatus of historical and theoretical positivism, to the "enigmas" which have always been the "general song" of creation. The true measure of *Canto general,* despite all the labors of Neruda to make it appear otherwise, is not to be found in a place name, an artifact, or an ideological loyalty—not in Stalingrad, Lota, or Macchu Picchu—but in the "havocs and bounties" of "El gran océano," the "shattering crescents" of "Leviathan," the "fullness of time" of "Los enigmas":

Probing a starry infinitude,

I came, like yourselves,
through the mesh of my being, in the night, and
    awoke to my nakedness,
all that was left of the catch—a fish in the
    noose of the wind.

(*Los enigmas*)

The present translation is offered in the spirit of this
conviction; and the accomplishment may be measured
accordingly. If the predicates of the "new method" urged
on translators by Mr. Stanley Burnshaw in *The Poem Itself*
are correct, the prevailing mood of translation is Parnas-
sian: it is possible now to be incredulous and close quotes
around the translator who *imagines* he is " 're-creating orig-
inals' "! In that case, fair warning may be more appropri-
ate for the conscientious translator than "apology": and the
reader is accordingly warned. These translations are tenta-
tive, illusionistic, and engaged. The myth of the omniscient
expositor and the univocal poem has had no part in the
shaping of this volume. Each word of the taxing originals,
and their English equivalents, has been prayerfully medi-
tated; yet commitment has exceeded meditation, in the
end—as it must, if the result is to be a translation rather
than a quandary. To keep up my courage under the as-
sault of an identity which might otherwise have proved
annihilating, I have mounted my language on rhythms
which enlist the resources of poetry in English as much as
they do the poetry of Pablo Neruda: I have worked at
objects. The stresses, at times, have carried me further from
the originals than I would have wished; and on certain
occasions the locutions of English have tidied the syntactical
disorders more than is proper. But the *Residencias* and the
Odas are no slagpile of words! The "poem itself" remains
where it always was—on "the other side of the page,"
where the bilingual are invited to consult it, unmediated:

by translators, by schoolteachers, by critics, by polemical methodists, and by other poets.

A word with regard to the selection of a text for the present volume. It should be obvious, in an *oeuvre* which already exceeds two thousand printed pages, and in which no fewer than six volumes, one of them "classic" in prestige and appeal, antedate the poet's twenty-second year, that a profile of sixty poems can hardly hope to "represent" the poet fairly. My hope has been to achieve the "representative" by other means: not by the simultaneous inclusion of set pieces from all of the volumes which comprise the complete works of Pablo Neruda, but by the projection of a diverse and mercurial talent in quest of its destiny. It has been the fate of that talent, during the last thirty-five years, to be truncated by partisan anthologists, diminished by causes, predilections, intrusions of history, injured by its own wilful insistence on allegiances which have little to do with the majesty and melancholy of its long contest with the Sphinx. There is need now to recover the true range of Neruda's labors as an agonist of the intuition: to peel away the politics, the patriotism, the provisional certainties, for that "interminable alcachofa" ("interminable artichoke") which he has called "the heart of all poets."

I say this with little hope of consoling connoisseurs in the "complete" Neruda, or devotees of any constituent part, for the omission of favorite epochs, like the youthful *Veinte poemas de amor y una canción desesperada* (*Twenty Love Poems and A Desperate Song*), and "indispensable" international landmarks like *Que despierte El Leñador!* (*Rail-Splitter, Awake!*) canonized by translation into the Arabian, Chinese, Slovenian, Czech, Hindu, German, French, Italian, Japanese, Russian, Polish, Rumanian, Ukrainian; and English (*Masses & Mainstream*: 1950). I offer in its place the projection of a poet working "at the right hand of power," and that poet's estimate of his true scope and commitment:

> A poetry impure as the clothing we wear, or our bodies, soup-stained, soiled with our shameful behavior, our wrinkles and vigils and dreams, observations and prophecies, declarations of loathing and love, idyls and beasts and shocks of encounter, political loyalties, denials and doubts, affirmations and taxes.

That is the order of business for a "selected poems of Neruda," and the desirable preponderance for a text. All are to be found in this volume.

I should like at this time to acknowledge the interest and counsel of friends who have helped to shape the direction of this book at phases crucial to its completion: to Dr. José F. Montesinos of the University of California, chiefly, who has patiently presided over my dilemmas since my first efforts in 1952; to Ángel del Río and Eugenio Florit, for timely favors of advice and intercession; and to Luis Monguió, for an appraisal of Neruda which should accomplish for English-speaking readers whatever the text of this translation has failed to achieve or omitted to undertake. My thanks are due the editors of *The Virginia Quarterly Review, The Nation, Stand* (London), and *Poetry* for permission to reprint translations first published in their pages; and in the case of *Poetry*, for portions of my Foreword originally published under the title of "Pablo Neruda and the Gigantesque" (1952).

—BEN BELITT

Bennington College,
Bennington, Vermont

Toward An
Impure Poetry

It is well, at certain hours of the day and night, to look closely at the world of objects at rest. Wheels that have crossed long, dusty distances with their mineral and vegetable burdens, sacks from the coalbins, barrels and baskets, handles and hafts for the carpenter's tool chest. From them flow the contacts of man with the earth, like a text for all harassed lyricists. The used surfaces of things, the wear that the hands give to things, the air, tragic at times, pathetic at others, of such things—all lend a curious attractiveness to the reality of the world that should not be underprized.

In them one sees the confused impurity of the human condition, the massing of things, the use and disuse of substances, footprints and fingerprints, the abiding presence of the human engulfing all artifacts, inside and out.

Let that be the poetry we search for: worn with the hand's obligations, as by acids, steeped in sweat and in smoke, smelling of lilies and urine, spattered diversely by the trades that we live by, inside the law or beyond it.

A poetry impure as the clothing we wear, or our bodies, soup-stained, soiled with our shameful behavior, our wrinkles and vigils and dreams, observations and prophecies, declarations of loathing and love, idyls and beasts, the shocks of encounter, political loyalties, denials and doubts, affirmations and taxes.

The holy canons of madrigal, the mandates of touch, smell, taste, sight, hearing, the passion for justice, sexual desire, the sea sounding—wilfully rejecting and accepting nothing: the deep penetration of things in the transports of love, a consummate poetry soiled by the pigeon's claw, ice-marked and tooth-marked, bitten delicately with our sweatdrops and usage, perhaps. Till the instrument played without respite yield us its solacing surfaces, and the wood show the thorniest suavities shaped by the pride of the tool. Blossom and water and wheat kernel share one precious consistency, the sumptuous appeal of the tactile.

Let no one forget them: despond, old mawkishness impure and unflawed, fruits of a fabulous species lost to the memory, cast away in a frenzy's abandonment—moonlight, the swan in the gathering darkness, all the hackneyed endearments: surely that is the poet's occasion, essential and absolute.

Those who shun the "bad taste" of things will fall on their face in the snow.

—PABLO NERUDA

Residencia en la Tierra / Residence on Earth
Series I, II, III
(1925-1945)

CABALLO DE LOS SUEÑOS

Innecesario, viéndome en los espejos,
con un gusto a semanas, a biógrafos, a papeles,
arranco de mi corazón al capitán del infierno,
establezco cláusulas indefinidamente tristes.

Vago de un punto a otro, absorbo ilusiones,
converso con los sastres en sus nidos:
ellos, a menudo, con voz fatal y fría
cantan y hacen huir los maleficios.

Hay un país extenso en el cielo
con las supersticiosas alfombras del arco-iris
y con vegetaciones vesperales:
hacia allí me dirijo, no sin cierta fatiga,
pisando una tierra removida de sepulcros un tanto frescos,
yo sueño entre esas plantas de legumbre confusa.

Paso entre documentos disfrutados, entre orígenes,
vestido como un ser original y abatido:
amo la miel gastada del respeto,
el dulce catecismo entre cuyas hojas
duermen violetas envejecidas, desvanecidas,
y las escobas, conmovedoras de auxilio:
en su apariencia hay, sin duda, pesadumbre y certeza.
Yo destruyo la rosa que silba y la ansiedad raptora:
yo rompo extremos queridos: y aun más,
aguardo el tiempo uniforme, sin medida:
un sabor que tengo en el alma me deprime.

DREAM HORSE

Needlessly, watching my looking-glass image,
with its passion for papers and cinemas, days of the week,
I pluck from my heart my hell's captain
and order the clauses, equivocally sad.

I drift between this point and that, absorbing illusions,
converse in the nests of the tailors:
sometimes the voices are glacial and deadly —
they sing, and the sorcery goes.

There's a country spread out in the sky,
a credulous carpet of rainbows
and crepuscular plants:
I move toward it just a bit haggardly,
trampling a gravedigger's rubble still moist from the spade
to dream in a bedlam of vegetables.

I walk between origins, beneficent documents,
chopfallen, dressed like a natural: I want
the spent honey of deference,
the sweets of the catechist under whose leaves
drained violets drowse and grow old;
and those bustling abettors, the brooms, in whose image,
assuredly, sorrow and certainty join.
I plunder the whistle of roses, the thieving anxiety:
I smash the attractive extremes—worst of all,
I await a symmetrical time beyond measure:
the taste of my spirit disheartens me.

Qué día ha sobrevenido! Qué espesa luz de leche,
compacta, digital, me favorece!
He oído relinchar su rojo caballo
desnudo sin herraduras y radiante.

Atravieso con él sobre las iglesias,
galopo los cuarteles desiertos de soldados
y un ejército impuro me persigue.
Sus ojos de eucaliptus roban sombra,
su cuerpo de campana galopa y golpea.

Yo necesito un relámpago de fulgor persistente,
un deudo festival que asuma mis herencias.

What a morning is here! What a milk-heavy glow
in the air, integral, all of a piece,
intending some good! I have heard its red horses,
naked to bridle and iron, shimmering, whinnying there.

Mounted, I soar over churches,
gallop the garrisons empty of soldiers
while a dissolute army pursues me.
Eucalyptus, its eyes raze the darkness
and the bell of its galloping body strikes home.

I need but a spark of that perduring brightness,
my jubilant kindred to claim my inheritance.

SABOR

De falsas astrologías, de costumbres un tanto lúgubres,
vertidas en lo inacabable y siempre llevadas al lado,
he conservado una tendencia, un sabor solitario.

De conversaciones gastadas como usadas maderas,
con humildad de sillas, con palabras ocupadas
en servir como esclavos de voluntad secundaria,
teniendo esa consistencia de la leche, de las semanas muertas,
del aire encadenado sobre las ciudades.

Quién puede jactarse de paciencia más sólida?
La cordura me envuelve de piel compacta
de un color reunido como una culebra:
mis criaturas nacen de un largo rechazo:
ay, con un solo alcohol puedo despedir este día
que he elegido, igual entre los días terrestres.

Vivo lleno de una substancia de color común, silenciosa
como una vieja madre, una paciencia fija
como sombra de iglesia o reposo de huesos.
Voy lleno de esas aguas dispuestas profundamente,
preparadas, durmiéndose en una atención triste.

En mi interior de guitarra hay un aire viejo,
seco y sonoro, permanecido, inmóvil,
como una nutrición fiel, como humo:
un elemento en descanso, un aceite vivo:
un pájaro de rigor cuida mi cabeza:
un ángel invariable vive en mi espada.

SAVOR

From counterfeit stargazers, somewhat maudlin proprieties,
from the flotsam of usage borne in on us always, close at
  hand,
inconclusive, I have cherished an impulse, a taste of my
  loneliness.

From table-talk flimsy as scrapwood,
with a chair's self-effacement and a language that labors
to wait on a substitute will, like a lackey,
milky in stamina, with last week's consistency,
stagnating in air, like smog on a city.

Who can boast a more tangible patience?
I am swathed in discretion, packed in like a hide
with a color that gathers itself to itself like a serpent.
All my creatures are born in a massive recoil;
one helping of alcohol—alas!—and I wave off the day
that I chose for myself, like all of the days of my world.

I live in the fullness of matter; my color is general;
mute as a matriarch, my forbearance is fixed
like a church and its shadow, or the quiet of bones.
I brim with the deep disposition of waters
primed and expectant, asleep in a lachrymose vigil.

The inner guitar that is I, keeps the catch of a ballad,
spare and sonorous, abiding, immobile,
like a punctual nutriment, like smoke in the air:
force in repose, the volatile power in the oil:
an incorruptible bird keeps watch on my head:
an unvarying angel inhabits my sword.

FANTASMA

Cómo surges de antaño, llegando,
encandilada, pálida estudiante,
a cuya voz aún piden consuelo
los meses dilatados y fijos.

Sus ojos luchaban como remeros
en el infinito muerto
con esperanza de sueño y materia
de seres saliendo del mar.

De la lejanía en donde
el olor de la tierra es otro
y lo vespertino llega llorando
en forma de oscuras amapolas.

En la altura de los días inmóviles
el insensible joven diurno
en tu rayo de luz se dormía
afirmado como en una espada.

Mientras tanto crece a la sombra
del largo transcurso en olvido
la flor de la soledad, húmeda, extensa,
como la tierra en un largo invierno.

FANTOM

How you rise from the past to me here,
pallid and wonderstruck schoolgirl,
at whose bidding the months, the fixed
and the lengthening months, turn for admonishment.

Your eyes struggled like oarsmen
in the perishing infinite
with a dream's expectation and the palpable
presences cast up by the sea.

Out of the faraway, where
the smell of the land is unplaceable
and twilight comes weeping
in a shadowy semblance of poppies.

Under daylight's immobile meridian,
daily the catalept drowsed, a child
in the blaze of your radiance,
insensate and proved, like a sword.

While deeper in shadow, from
the leisurely lapse of oblivion,
the flower of your solitude, tumid in earth
like a lengthening winter, grows ample.

COLECCIÓN NOCTURNA

He vencido al ángel del sueño, el funesto alegórico:
su gestión insistía, su denso paso llega
envuelto en caracoles y cigarras,
marino, perfumado de frutos agudos.

Es el viento que agita los meses, el silbido de un tren,
el paso de la temperatura sobre el lecho,
un opaco sonido de sombra
que cae como trapo en lo interminable,
una repetición de distancias, un vino de color confundido,
un paso polvoriento de vacas bramando.

A veces su canasto negro cae en mi pecho,
sus sacos de dominio hieren mi hombro,
su multitud de sal, su ejército entreabierto
recorren y revuelven las cosas del cielo:
él galopa en la respiración y su paso es de beso:
su salitre seguro planta en los párpados
con vigor esencial y solemne propósito:
entra en lo preparado como un dueño:
su substancia sin ruido equipa de pronto,
su alimento profético propaga tenazmente.

Reconozco a menudo sus guerreros,
sus piezas corroídas por el aire, sus dimensiones,
y su necesidad de espacio es tan violenta
que baja hasta mi corazón a buscarlo:
él es el propietario de las mesetas inaccesibles,
él baila con personajes trágicos y cotidianos:
de noche rompe mi piel su ácido aéreo
y escucho en mi interior temblar su instrumento.

NOCTURNAL COLLECTION

I had vanquished that angel of sleep, allegorical
mourner; but his travail went on and his ponderous footfall
came closer, sheathed with snails and cicadas,
sea-born, and brackish, smelling of fruits.

Wind rattles the months, a train whistles,
fever paces the bedposts,
a hard intonation of darkness,
like a bottomless downfall of patches,
distance repeated, wine in a nondescript color,
the dusty approach and the bawling of cows.

Sometimes the black of his basket falls hard on my chest,
his conqueror's pack cuts my shoulder—
all his legions of brine, the armies deploying by halves
overturning the heavens, overtaking the things of the sky:
his breathing goes at a gallop, his step is a kiss:
his infallible salts bind the eye
with the might of their essences, his somber intent:
he enters his providence there like a master
soundlessly robed in his substances, suddenly whole;
he engenders prophetical foods, without quarter.

His campaigners have often been known to me,
with their weapons corroding in air, their immensity:
so savage their passion for space,
he has harried my heart's depths in search of it:
he rules the uncharted plateaus,
has danced with the doomed and the usual.
His aerial acids break into my flesh in the night
and I hear in my entrails his instrument stir.

Pablo Neruda / 51

Yo oigo el sueño de viejos compañeros y mujeres amadas,
sueños cuyos latidos me quebrantan:
su material de alfombra piso en silencio,
su luz de amapola muerdo con delirio.
Cadáveres dormidos que a menudo
danzan asidos al peso de mi corazón,
qué ciudades opacas recorremos!

Mi pardo corcel de sombra se agiganta,
y sobre envejecidos tahures, sobre lenocinios de escaleras
    gastadas,
sobre lechos de niñas desnudas, entre jugadores de football,
del viento ceñidos pasamos:
y entonces caen a nuestra boca esos frutos blandos del cielo,
los pájaros, las campanas conventuales, los cometas:
aquel que se nutrió de geografía pura y estremecimiento,
ése tal vez nos vió pasar centelleando.

Camaradas cuyas cabezas reposan sobre barriles,
en un desmantelado buque prófugo, lejos,
amigos míos sin lágrimas, mujeres de rostro cruel:
la medianoche ha llegado y un gong de muerte
golpea en torno mío como el mar.
Hay en la boca el sabor, la sal del dormido.
Fiel como una condena, a cada cuerpo
la palidez del distrito letárgico acude:
una sonrisa fría, sumergida,
unos ojos cubiertos como fatigados boxeadores,
una respiración que sordamente devora fantasmas.

En esa humedad de nacimiento, con esa proporción te-
    nebrosa,
cerrada como una bodega, el aire es criminal:
las paredes tienen un triste color de cocodrilo,
una contextura de araña siniestra:

I listen: for a dream of old playfellows, women beloved,
and am rent by the shock of my dreaming.
Speechless I tread on the pile of the carpets
or bite on the blaze of his poppy, transported.
O you slumbering dead who so often
have danced with me, caught to the weight of my heart,
toward what lusterless cities we journey!

My shadow-horse swarthily masses its bulk:
we pass over crumbling casinos, pimps on the ruining stair,
girls bedded down naked, football professionals
encircled by wind:
a velvety fruit falls into our mouths from the sky,
comets and birds and conventual bells:
only those who grow fat on geometry, perfect and
     tremulous,
it may be, saw us twinkle in passing.

Bully-boys with your heads on a barrel top,
in a castaway vessel, dismantled and distant,
friends who live dry-eyed, and flint-featured ladies:
it is midnight: all around me
death beats on a gong, like the sea.
An aftertaste stays in my mouth: the brine of the sleeper.
Certain as judgment, condemning us each in our bones,
the kingdoms of lethargy rise in their pallor:
a frozen smile drowning,
the eyes taking cover, like a boxer's exhaustion,
dumbly dispelling a ghost with our breathing.

So, with the damp of this birth pang, with this shadowy
     symmetry
like a wine cellar padlocked, the air, too, is criminal.
Sad crocodile colors the wall
and the sinister weft of the spider:

se pisa en lo blando como sobre un monstruo muerto:
las uvas negras inmensas, repletas,
cuelgan de entre las ruinas como odres:

oh Capitán, en nuestra hora de reparto
abre los mudos cerrojos y espérame:
allí debemos cenar vestidos de luto:
el enfermo de malaria guardará las puertas.
Mi corazón, es tarde y sin orillas,
el día, como un pobre mantel puesto a secar,
oscila rodeado de seres y extensión:
de cada ser viviente hay algo en la atmósfera:
mirando mucho el aire aparecerían mendigos,
abogados, bandidos, carteros, costureras,
y un poco de cada oficio, un resto humillado
quiere trabajar su parte en nuestro interior.
Yo busco desde antaño, yo examino sin arrogancia,
conquistado, sin duda, por lo vespertino.

we tread over pulp like a carrion monster:
black grapes hang enormous, a bloating of juices,
clogging the ruins like wineskins.

Captain, whatever our reckoning
slip the mute latchets and wait for me there:
We must feast in our funeral clothing:
a malarial patient stands watch by the doors.
Love, it grows late, and the shorelines are lost.
A day like a tatter of tablecloth drying
flaps in a circle of lives and extension.
All things that live give some part of themselves to the air.
Intent upon atmosphere, keeping close watch, come the
    beggars,
the lawyers, the gangsters, the postmen, the sempstresses:
a little of every vocation, a humbled remainder
that works toward some destined completion within us.
I have looked for it long—vanquished, no doubt,
by the evenings—and go on with no arrogance.

ARTE POÉTICA

Entre sombra y espacio, entre guarniciones y doncellas,
dotado de corazón singular y sueños funestos,
precipitadamente pálido, marchito en la frente
y con luto de viudo furioso por cada día de vida,
ay, para cada agua invisible que bebo soñolientamente
y de todo sonido que acojo temblando,
tengo la misma sed ausente y la misma fiebre fría,
un oído que nace, una angustia indirecta,
como si llegaran ladrones o fantasmas,
y en una cáscara de extensión fija y profunda,
como un camarero humillado, como una campana un poco
    ronca,
como un espejo viejo, como un olor de casa sola
en la que los huéspedes entran de noche perdidamente
    ebrios,
y hay un olor de ropa tirada al suelo, y una ausencia de
    flores,
—posiblemente de otro modo aún menos melancólico—,
pero, la verdad, de pronto, el viento que azota mi pecho,
las noches de substancia infinita caídas en mi dormitorio,
el ruido de un día que arde con sacrificio
me piden lo profético que hay en mí, con melancolía,
y un golpe de objetos que llaman sin ser respondidos
hay, y un movimiento sin tregua, y un nombre confuso.

ARS POETICA

Between dark and the void, between virgins and garrisons,
with my singular heart and my mournful conceits
for my portion, my forehead despoiled, overtaken by pallors,
a grief-maddened widower bereft of a lifetime;
for every invisible drop that I taste in a stupor, alas,
for each intonation I concentrate, shuddering,
I keep the identical thirst of an absence, the identical chill
of a fever; sounds, coming to be; a devious anguish
as of thieves and chimeras approaching;
so, in the shell of extension, profound and unaltering,
demeaned as a kitchen-drudge, like a bell sounding
    hoarsely,
like a tarnishing mirror, or the smell of a house's abandon-
    ment
where the guests stagger homeward, blind drunk, in the
    night,
and the reek of their clothes rises out of the floor, an absence
    of flowers—
could it be differently put, a little less ruefully, possibly?—
All the truth blurted out: wind strikes at my breast like a
    blow,
the ineffable body of night, fallen into my bedroom,
the roar of a morning ablaze with some sacrifice,
that begs my prophetical utterance, mournfully;
an impact of objects that call and encounter no answer,
unrest without respite, an anomalous name.

COMUNICACIONES DESMENTIDAS

Aquellos días extraviaron mi sentido profético, a mi casa
entraban los coleccionistas de sellos, y emboscados, a altas
horas de la estación, asaltaban mis cartas, arrancaban de ellas
besos frescos, besos sometidos a una larga residencia marina,
y conjuros que protegían mi suerte con ciencia femenina y
defensiva caligrafía.

Vivía al lado de otras casas, otras personas y árboles ten-
diendo a lo grandioso, pabellones de follaje pasional, raíces
emergidas, palas vegetales, cocoteros directos, y, en medio
de estas espumas verdes, pasaba con mi sombrero puntiagudo
y un corazón por completo novelesco, con tranco pesado de
esplendor, porque a medida que mis poderes se roían, y
destruídos en polvo buscaban simetría como los muertos en
los cementerios, los lugares conocidos, las extensiones hasta
esa hora despreciadas y los rostros que como plantas lentas
brotaban en mi abandono, variaban a mi alrededor con terror
y sigilo, como cantidades de hojas que un otoño súbito
trastorna.

Loros, estrellas, y además el sol oficial y una brusca hume-
dad hicieron nacer en mí un gusto ensimismado por la tierra
y cuanta cosa la cubría, y una satisfacción de casa vieja por
sus murciélagos, una delicadeza de mujer desnuda por sus
uñas, dispusieron en mí como de armas débiles y tenaces de
mis facultades vergonzosas, y la melancolía puso su estría en
mi tejido, y la carta de amor, pálida de papel y temor, sus-
trajo su araña trémula que apenas teje y sin cesar desteje y
teje. Naturalmente, de la luz lunar, de su circunstancial pro-
longación, y más aún, de su eje frío, que los pájaros (golon-
drinas, ocas) no pueden pisar ni en los delirios de la emigra-
ción, de su piel azul, lisa, delgada y sin alhajas, caí hacia el

FALSIFIED DOCUMENTS

In days that deceived my prophetical genius, philatelists entered my house, and lying in wait until late at my post, they assaulted my letters, ungummed the cold kisses, kisses addressed to a seaside chalet, and the talismans warding my luck with a feminine science, a defensive calligraphy.

I lived in a cluster of houses, among people and trees and a noble perspective: pavilions of passional leafage, roots breaking the subsoil, plants bladed like oars, immediate coconut palms; and there in the midst of a spindrift of verdure, I moved with my sharp-pointed hat, my heart a pure fiction, my stride heavy with splendors; for however my virtues declined or sought out their shapes in the dust, like the dead in their graveyards, demolished, the habitual scene, the sum of the spaces disdained till that hour, the faces like gradual plants blossomed into my loneliness, multiplied terror and secrecy around me like a bulking of leaves suddenly shocked by an autumn.

Laurel and stars, a sanction of subsequent sun and a bristling humidity, quickened my studious taste for the soil and all that adorns it; content as a ruined old house with its slime or the finicking nude with her fingernails, they planted themselves in my bones—ineffectual weapons still stubbornly joined to my profligate faculties; melancholias dinted my substance with furrows; and a love letter, pallid with paper and panic, arrested its tremulous spider, that barely could weave and unweave and weave its web endlessly over. Easily, out of the moonlight—its explicit projections, and beyond, from the freeze of its axis—so that even the birds (the swallow, the goose) need not tread on that frenzied migration, out of the blues of that flesh,

Pablo Neruda / 59

duelo, como quien cae herido de arma blanca. Yo soy sujeto de sangre especial, y esa substancia a la vez nocturna y marítima me hacía alterar y padecer, y esas aguas subcelestes degradaban mi energía y lo comercial de mi disposición.

De ese modo histórico mis huesos adquirieron gran preponderancia en mis intenciones: el reposo, las mansiones a la orilla del mar me atraían sin seguridad pero con destino, y una vez llegado al recinto, rodeado del coro mudo y más inmóvil, sometido a la hora postrera y sus perfumes, injusto con las geografías inexactas y partidario mortal del sillón de cemento, aguardo el tiempo militarmente, y con el florete de la aventura manchado de sangre olvidada.

unadorned and emaciate, I fell into my sorrows, as if hurt by the white of a weapon. I live bound to a singular blood: an ichor, nocturnal and tidal at once, presides on my changes and agonies; and all of the waters that flow under heaven diminish my force and the marks of my nature.

By modes as historic as this, my preponderant bones took the weight of my purposes: some dream of repose, of mansions that give on the seacoast, worked with a fateful attraction, uncertainly; drawn into those closures, ringed by that mute and most motionless chorus, constrained to that ultimate hour and its perfumes, wronged by the faulty geographies and the mortal well-wishers cemented in armchairs, I keep militant watch upon time, the foils of my hazard still stained with oblivious blood.

ENTIERRO EN EL ESTE

Yo trabajo de noche, rodeado de ciudad,
de pescadores, de alfareros, de difuntos quemados
con azafrán y frutas, envueltos en muselina escarlata:
bajo mi balcón esos muertos terribles
pasan sonando cadenas y flautas de cobre,
estridentes y finas y lúgubres silban
entre el color de las pesadas flores envenenadas
y el grito de los cenicientos danzarines
y el creciente monótono de los tamtam
y el humo de las maderas que arden y huelen.

Porque una vez doblado el camino, junto al turbio río,
sus corazones, detenidos o iniciando un mayor movimiento,
rodarán quemados, con la pierna y el pie hechos fuego,
y la trémula ceniza caerá sobre el agua,
flotará como ramo de flores calcinadas
o como extinto fuego dejado por tan poderosos viajeros
que hicieron arder algo sobre las negras aguas, y devoraron
un aliento desaparecido y un licor extremo.

BURIAL IN THE EAST

I work nights, in the ring of the city,
among fisherfolk, potters, cadavers, cremations
of saffron and fruits shrouded into red muslin.
Under my balcony pass the terrible dead
sounding their coppery flutes and their chains,
strident and mournful and delicate—they hiss
in a blazon of poisoned and ponderous flowers,
through the cries of the smoldering dancers,
the tom-tom's augmented monotony,
in the crackle and fume of the woodsmoke.

One turn in the road, by the ooze of the river,
and their hearts, clogging up or preparing some monstrous
    exertion,
will whirl away burning, their legs and their feet incan-
    descent;
the tremulous ash will descend on the water
and float like a branching of carbonized flowers—
a bonfire put out by the might of some wayfarer
who lighted the black of the water and devoured some part
of a vanished subsistence, a consummate libation.

CABALLERO SOLO

Los jóvenes homosexuales y las muchachas amorosas,
y las largas viudas que sufren el delirante insomnio,
y las jóvenes señoras preñadas hace treinta horas,
y los roncos gatos que cruzan mi jardín en tinieblas,
como un collar de palpitantes ostras sexuales
rodean mi residencia solitaria,
como enemigos establecidos contra mi alma,
como conspiradores en traje de dormitorio
que cambiaran largos besos espesos por consigna.

El radiante verano conduce a los enamorados
en uniformes regimientos melancólicos,
hechos de gordas y flacas y alegres y tristes parejas:
bajo los elegantes cocoteros, junto al océano y la luna,
hay una continua vida de pantalones y polleras,
un rumor de medias de seda acariciadas,
y senos femeninos que brillan como ojos.

El pequeño empleado, después de mucho,
después del tedio semanal, y las novelas leídas de noche en
    cama,
ha definitivamente seducido a su vecina,
y la lleva a los miserables cinematógrafos
donde los héroes son potros o príncipes apasionados,
y acaricia sus piernas llenas de dulce vello
con sus ardientes y húmedas manos que huelen a cigarrillo.

Los atardeceres del seductor y las noches de los esposos
se unen como dos sábanas sepultándome,
y las horas después del almuerzo en que los jóvenes
    estudiantes

GENTLEMAN ALONE

The young homosexuals and languishing girls,
the tall widows frantic with sleeplessness,
the matrons still tender in years, now thirty hours pregnant,
the gravel-voiced tomcats that cross in the night of my
  garden
like a necklace of sensual oysters, atremble,
encircle my lonely environs—
antagonists stalking my soul,
schemers in nightgowns,
exchanging long kisses, packed in like a countersign.

The luminous summer leads on: formations
of lovers identically sad,
deploying in twos: the lean with the plump, the merry and
  mournful:
under elegant coconut palms, near the moon and the ocean,
the bustle of trousers and petticoat-hoops is unending,
a sound of silk hosiery fondled,
and the feminine nipple blazing out like an eye.

At long last, the petty employee, delivered from weekly
routine, after bedding himself for the night with a novel,
seduces his neighbor conclusively.
They go on to a villainous movie
where all of the heroes are horses or passionate princes,
and he dandles a fleecy pubescence of legs
with his sweltering fingers still rank with tobacco.

All the twilight seducers, the nights of the wedded,
close over like bed sheets and bury me:
all those hours after luncheon, when the green undergrad-
  uate,

Pablo Neruda / 65

y las jóvenes estudiantes, y los sacerdotes se ma'turban,
y los animales fornican directamente,
y las abejas huelen a sangre, y las moscas zumban coléricas,
y los primos juegan extrañamente con sus primas,
y los médicos miran con furia al marido de la joven paciente,
y las horas de la mañana en que el profesor, como por
    descuido,
cumple con su deber conyugal y desayuna,
y más aún, los adúlteros, que se aman con verdadero amor
sobre lechos altos y largos como embarcaciones:
seguramente, eternamente me rodea
este gran bosque respiratorio y enredado
con grandes flores como bocas y dentaduras
y negras raíces en forma de uñas y zapatos.

the boys and the girls, and the ministers, masturbate,
and the beasts couple openly;
when the bee sniffs a blood-smell, the choleric fly
buzzes, the cousin plays games with his girl-cousin
queerly; when the doctor keeps furious watch on the mate
    of the lady
malingerer; the matutinal hour when the schoolteacher
absentmindedly renders his conjugal due and sits down to
    his breakfast;
above all, the adulterers making love with unfalsified
ardor, on bedsteads like boats, high and trim on the waters:
so, tautly, eternally,
that big, breathing forest encircles me
with its raddle of towering blossoms, like mouths with
    their teeth:
it is black at the root; it is shaped like a shoe and a finger-
    nail.

Largamente he permanecido mirando mis largas piernas,
con ternura infinita y curiosa, con mi acostumbrada pasión,
como si hubieran sido las piernas de una mujer divina
profundamente sumida en el abismo de mi tórax:
y es que, la verdad, cuando el tiempo, el tiempo pasa,
sobre la tierra, sobre el techo, sobre mi impura cabeza,
y pasa, el tiempo pasa, y en mi lecho no siento de noche
    que una mujer está respirando, durmiendo desnuda y
    a mi lado,
entonces, extrañas, oscuras cosas toman el lugar de la
    ausente,
viciosos, melancólicos pensamientos
siembran pesadas posibilidades en mi dormitorio,
y así, pues, miro mis piernas como si pertenecieran a otro
    cuerpo,
y fuerte y dulcemente estuvieran pegadas a mis entrañas.

Como tallos o femeninas, adorables cosas,
desde las rodillas suben, cilíndricas y espesas,
con turbado y compacto material de existencia:
como brutales, gruesos brazos de diosa,
como árboles monstruosamente vestidos de seres humanos,
como fatales, inmensos labios sedientos y tranquilos,
son allí la mejor parte de mi cuerpo:
lo enteramente substancial, sin complicado contenido
de sentidos o tráqueas o intestinos o ganglios:
nada, sino lo puro, lo dulce y espeso de mi propia vida,
nada, sino la forma y el volumen existiendo,
guardando la vida, sin embargo, de una manera completa.

For a long while I've pondered them now—these big legs
of mine:
with infinite tenderness, curious, with my usual passion—
as if they belonged to a stranger, some miraculous beauty
planted deep in the well of my thorax.
Truth is, as time passes and passes,
passes over the earth and the roof and my dissolute head,
time
passing and passing, at length, in my bed, it seems some-
thing more than a woman is breathing, sleeping nude at
my side.
Things odd and occult change place with an absent illusion;
thoughts morbid or mournful
that scatter the weight of the possible over my bedroom
like pollen:
and it happens I stare at my legs as if they were joined to
some bulk never really my own,
trimly and powerfully thrust in my entrails, with a blow.

Like stalks, like some winsome and feminine thing,
they climb from my knees, compact and cylindrical,
tight with the turbulent stuff of my life:
brutish and lubberly, like the arms of a goddess,
like trees monstrously clad in the guise of the human,
like vast and malevolent lips, athirst and immobile,
all the heft of my body waits there:
the sum of the substantive, bald, with no burden of rec-
ondite meanings,
no trachea, ganglia, viscera—
all that is purest and sweetest and gross in my singular be-
ing:
nothing but volume and form, in extension,
keeping watch on my life, none the less, with a perfect
solicitude.

Pablo Neruda / 69

Las gentes cruzan el mundo en la actualidad
sin apenas recordar que poseen un cuerpo y en él la vida,
y hay miedo, hay miedo en el mundo de las palabras que
   designan el cuerpo,
y se habla favorablemente de la ropa,
de pantalones es posible hablar, de trajes,
y de ropa interior de mujer (de medias y ligas de "señora"),
como si por las calles fueran las prendas y los trajes vacíos
   por completo
y un oscuro y obsceno guardarropas ocupara el mundo.

Tienen existencia los trajes, color, forma, designio,
y profundo lugar en nuestros mitos, demasiado lugar,
demasiados muebles y demasiadas habitaciones hay en el
   mundo,
y mi cuerpo vive entre y bajo tantas cosas abatido,
con un pensamiento fijo de esclavitud y de cadenas.

Bueno, mis rodillas, como nudos,
particulares, funcionarios, evidentes,
separan las mitades de mis piernas en forma seca:
y en realidad dos mundos diferentes, dos sexos diferentes
no son tan diferentes como las dos mitades de mis piernas.

Desde la rodilla hasta el pie una forma dura,
mineral, fríamente útil, aparece,
una criatura de hueso y persistencia,
y los tobillos no son ya sino el propósito desnudo,
la exactitud y lo necesario dispuestos en definitiva.

Others travel the tangible world
with no thought for their bodies, barely aware of its
    vigors:
fear walks the world of the words which pertain to our
    bodies—there is fear—
as we chatter and sanction our clothing
and speak about trousers and suits with abandon,
or of lingerie ("ladies' " garters and hosiery)
as if business suits, utterly emptied, walked abroad in the
    streets, haberdashery,
and the rest of the world were a clothespress, benighted
    and bestial.

Clothes have their existence: they have colors and patterns
    and forms,
and live deep—far too deep!—in our myths;
there is too much shelter and furniture loose in the world,
while the flesh lives defamed, in a welter of scurrilous
    things,
underneath, obsessed with its thralldom, in chains.

Take these knees of mine: manifest,
functional, private, like knots,
dividing the halves of my legs, in their crisp conformation:
two kingdoms distinct in themselves, two differing sexes,
are no less unlike than the halves of my legs.

Down from the knee to the foot—a tangible integer,
mineral, coolly available, appears
in a creaturely image of bones and persistence:
the ankles like pure resolution,
precise and essential, pursuing its will to the close.

Sin sensualidad, cortas y duras, y masculinas,
son allí mis piernas, y dotadas
de grupos musculares como animales complementarios,
y allí también una vida, una sólida, sutil, aguda vida
sin temblar permanece, aguardando y actuando.

En mis pies cosquillosos,
y duros como el sol, y abiertos como flores,
y perpetuos, magníficos soldados
en la guerra gris del espacio,
todo termina, la vida termina definitivamente en mis pies,
lo extranjero y lo hostil allí comienza:
los nombres del mundo, lo fronterizo y lo remoto,
lo sustantivo y lo adjetivo que no caben en mi corazón
con densa y fría constancia allí se originan.

Siempre,
productos manufacturados, medias, zapatos,
o simplemente aire infinito.
Habrá entre mis pies y la tierra
extremando lo aislado y lo solitario de mi ser,
algo tenazmente supuesto entre mi vida y la tierra,
algo abiertamente invencible y enemigo.

And those legs, there, my masculine legs,
unsensual, bluff, and resilient; endowed
with their clustering muscles, complementary animals—
they, too, are a life, a substantial and delicate world,
alert and unfaltering, living watchful and strenuous there.

So, to the ticklish extremes of my footsoles,
stanch as the sun, and expanded like flowers,
a troop in the wan wars of space, unflagging, resplendent—
all come to an end, all that is living concludes in my feet:
from there on, the hostile and alien begins:
all the names of the world, outposts and frontiers,
the noun and its adjective that my heart never summoned
compact with consistency, coolly, emerge.

Always
things, fabrications: stockings and shoes,
or simply the infinite air:
dividing my feet from the dust of the world,
compelling my solitude, compounding my exile:
between life and the earth that I tread, the assumption,
    unyieldingly there,
the invincible power and the enemy agent, laid bare.

SIGNIFICA SOMBRAS

Qué esperanza considerar, qué presagio puro,
qué definitivo beso enterrar en el corazón,
someter en los orígenes del desamparo y la inteligencia,
suave y seguro sobre las aguas eternamente turbadas?

Qué vitales, rápidas alas de un nuevo ángel de sueños
instalar en mis hombros dormidos para seguridad perpetua,
de tal manera que el camino entre las estrellas de la muerte
sea un violento vuelo comenzado desde hace muchos días
      y meses y siglos?

Tal vez la debilidad natural de los seres recelosos y ansiosos
busca de súbito permanencia en el tiempo y límites en la
      tierra,
tal vez las fatigas y las edades acumuladas implacablemente
se extiendan como la ola lunar de un océano recién creado
sobre litorales y tierras angustiosamente desiertas.

Ay, que lo que yo soy siga existiendo y cesando de existir,
y que mi obediencia se ordene con tales condiciones de
      hierro
que el temblor de las muertes y de los nacimientos no
      conmueva
el profundo sitio que quiero reservar para mí eternamente.

Sea, pues, lo que soy, en alguna parte y en todo tiempo,
establecido y asegurado y ardiente testigo,
cuidadosamente destruyéndose y preservándose
      incesantemente,
evidentemente empeñado en su deber original.

SIGNIFYING SHADOWS

What hope shall we cherish, what pure premonition,
what definitive kiss shall we plant in our hearts
or confide to the source of our wit and our indolence,
supple and certain, on the waters' abiding inquietude?

What ardent and hurrying wing of that unforseen angel
commanding our sleep shall feather my dream, for a change-
    less security,
that my path between death and the stars be a vehement
flight into air, whose beginning is ageless: a day or a month
    or an eon?

Is it a human defect of our haunted and fainthearted lives
that we ask for a sudden persistence in time, in the com-
    pass of matter?
Or a weariness, maybe—the compounding of ages that
    open implacably
outward: a latter-day deluge working under the moon,
heartsick, in a desert of beaches and rubble?

Oh that the thing that is I, might persist in its being and
    ceasing
to be; that my sufferance might order itself with such iron
conditions that the spasms of dying and the throes of be-
    ginning
leave the fathoms I keep for my portion, untroubled!

Whatever my singular self, in some part of me, always
to continue, a sedulous witness confirmed in my being, un-
    shaken,
forever unmaking and making identity, warily,
fast in my promises, all my pledges made manifest.

Pablo Neruda / 75

WALKING AROUND

Sucede que me canso de ser hombre.
Sucede que entro en las sastrerías y en los cines
marchito, impenetrable, como un cisne de fieltro
navegando en un agua de origen y ceniza.

El olor de las peluquerías me hace llorar a gritos.
Sólo quiero un descanso de piedras o de lana,
sólo quiero no ver establecimientos ni jardines,
ni mercaderías, ni anteojos, ni ascensores.

Sucede que me canso de mis pies y mis uñas
y mi pelo y mi sombra.
Sucede que me canso de ser hombre.

Sin embargo sería delicioso
asustar a un notario con un lirio cortado
o dar muerte a una monja con un golpe de oreja.
Sería bello
ir por las calles con un cuchillo verde
y dando gritos hasta morir de frío.

No quiero seguir siendo raíz en las tinieblas,
vacilante, extendido, tiritando de sueño,
hacia abajo, en las tripas mojadas de la tierra,
absorbiendo y pensando, comiendo cada día.

No quiero para mí tantas desgracias.
No quiero continuar de raíz y de tumba,

WALKING AROUND

It so happens I'm tired of just being a man.
I go to a movie, drop in at the tailor's—it so happens—
feeling wizened and numbed, like a big, wooly swan,
awash on an ocean of clinkers and causes.

A whiff from a barbershop does it: I yell bloody murder.
All I ask is a little vacation from things: from boulders and
    woolens,
from gardens, institutional projects, merchandise,
eyeglasses, elevators—I'd rather not look at them.

It so happens I'm fed—with my feet and my fingernails
and my hair and my shadow.
Being a man leaves me cold: that's how it is.

Still—it would be lovely
to wave a cut lily and panic a notary,
or finish a nun with a left to the ear.
It would be nice
just to walk down the street with a green switchblade
    handy,
whooping it up till I die of the shivers.

I won't live like this—like a root in a shadow,
wide-open and wondering, teeth chattering sleepily,
going down to the dripping entrails of the universe
absorbing things, taking things in, eating three squares a
    day.

I've had all I'll take from catastrophe.
I won't have it this way, muddling through like a root or a
    grave,

Pablo Neruda / 77

de subterráneo solo, de bodega con muertos,
aterido, muriéndome de pena.

Por eso el día lunes arde como el petróleo
cuando me ve llegar con mi cara de cárcel,
y aúlla en su transcurso como una rueda herida,
y da pasos de sangre caliente hacia la noche.

Y me empuja a ciertos rincones, a ciertas casas húmedas,
a hospitales donde los huesos salen por la ventana,
a ciertas zapaterías con olor a vinagre,
a calles espantosas como grietas.

Hay pájaros de color de azufre y horribles intestinos
colgando de las puertas de las casas que odio,
hay dentaduras olvidadas en una cafetera,
hay espejos
que debieran haber llorado de vergüenza y espanto,
hay paraguas en todas partes, y venenos, y ombligos.

Yo paseo con calma, con ojos, con zapatos,
con furia, con olvido,
paso, cruzo oficinas y tiendas de ortopedia,
y patios donde hay ropas colgadas de un alambre:
calzoncillos, toallas y camisas que lloran
lentas lágrimas sucias.

all alone underground, in a morgue of cadavers,
cold as a stiff, dying of misery.

That's why Monday flares up like an oil-slick,
when it sees me up close, with the face of a jailbird,
or squeaks like a broken-down wheel as it goes,
stepping hot-blooded into the night.

Something shoves me toward certain damp houses, into
    certain dark corners,
into hospitals, with bones flying out of the windows;
into shoe stores and shoemakers smelling of vinegar,
streets frightful as fissures laid open.

There, trussed to the doors of the houses I loathe
are the sulphurous birds, in a horror of tripes,
dental plates lost in a coffeepot,
mirrors
that must surely have wept with the nightmare and shame
    of it all;
and everywhere, poisons, umbrellas, and belly buttons.

I stroll unabashed, in my eyes and my shoes
and my rage and oblivion.
I go on, crossing offices, retail orthopedics,
courtyards with laundry hung out on a wire:
the blouses and towels and the drawers newly washed,
slowly dribbling a slovenly tear.

ODA CON UN LAMENTO

Oh niña entre las rosas, oh presión de palomas,
oh presidio de peces y rosales,
tu alma es una botella llena de sal sedienta
y una campana llena de uvas es tu piel.

Por desgracia no tengo para darte sino uñas
o pestañas, o pianos derretidos,
o sueños que salen de mi corazón a borbotones,
polvorientos sueños que corren como jinetes negros,
sueños llenos de velocidades y desgracias.

Sólo puedo quererte con besos y amapolas,
con guirnaldas mojadas por la lluvia,
mirando cenicientos caballos y perros amarillos.

Sólo puedo quererte con olas a la espalda,
entre vagos golpes de azufre y aguas ensimismadas,
nadando en contra de los cementerios que corren en
    ciertos ríos
con pasto mojado creciendo sobre las tristes tumbas de yeso,
nadando a través de corazones sumergidos
y pálidas planillas de niños insepultos.
Hay mucha muerte, muchos acontecimientos funerarios
en mis desamparadas pasiones y desolados besos,
hay el agua que cae en mi cabeza,
mientras crece mi pelo,
un agua como el tiempo, un agua negra desencadenada,
con una voz nocturna, con un grito
de pájaro en la lluvia, con una interminable
sombra de ala mojada que protege mis huesos:
mientras me visto, mientras

ODE WITH A LAMENT

O girl among the roses, excitation of doves,
O fortress of fishes and rosebushes,
your soul is a flask of dried salts
and your skin is a bell full of grapes.

I come with no presents, unluckily—only
fingernails, eyelashes, melted pianos,
with dreams bubbling out of my breast,
powdery dreams like a flight of black horsemen,
dreams full of haste and calamity.

Only with kisses and poppies can I love you,
with rain-sodden wreaths,
as I brood on the ash of the horse and the yellow of dogs.

Only with waves at my back can I love you:
in the dubious clashing of sulphur and preoccupied water
I swim up the current, past the graveyards afloat on those
    rivers,
watery pastures that feed on the lachrymose chalk of the
    tombs;
I countercross hearts under water,
wan birth dates of children bereft of their burials.
So much dying, such an endless necrology
in my destitute passions, my desolate kisses!
The waters are loosed on my head
while my forelock grows longer—
water like time breaking free of itself, black water
like a voice in the night, like the screaming
of birds in the rain, an interminable
darkness of wings wetted down, keeping watch on my bones
while I dress, while

interminablemente me miro en los espejos y en los vidrios,
oigo que alguien me sigue llamándome a sollozos
con una triste voz podrida por el tiempo.

Tú estás de pie sobre la tierra, llena
de dientes y relámpagos.
Tú propagas los besos y matas las hormigas.
Tú lloras de salud, de cebolla, de abeja,
de abecedario ardiendo.
Tú eres como una espada azul y verde
y ondulas al tocarte, como un río.

Ven a mi alma vestida de blanco, con un ramo
de ensangrentadas rosas y copas de cenizas,
ven con una manzana y un caballo,
porque allí hay una sala oscura y un candelabro roto,
unas sillas torcidas que esperan el invierno,
y una paloma muerta, con un número.

I endlessly study my image in mirror and window glass
and hear the pursuers still sobbing and calling my name
in a woebegone voice fouled with time.

You stand tall on your feet above ground, full
of teeth and the lightning.
You propagate kisses and deal death to the ant.
You moan with well-being, with the bee and the onion,
you catch fire from a page of your primer.
You are all green and blue, like a sword blade,
and you weave to my touch, like a river.

Come into my soul, dressed in white, like a branch
of blood-roses, like a chalice of ashes.
Come close with a horse and an apple:
there the sitting room waits in the dark, with a smashed
    candelabrum,
till it be winter; a few twisted chairs
and a dead dove with a band and a number.

2. *Apogeo del Apio*

Del centro puro que los ruidos nunca
atravesaron, de la intacta cera,
salen claros relámpagos lineales,
palomas con destino de volutas,
hacia tardías calles con olor
a sombra y a pescado.

Son las venas del apio! Son la espuma, la risa,
los sombreros del apio!
Son los signos del apio, su sabor
de luciérnaga, sus mapas
de color inundado,
y cae su cabeza ángel verde,
y sus delgados rizos se acongojan,
y entran los pies del apio en los mercados
de la mañana herida, entre sollozos,
y se cierran las puertas a su paso,
y los dulces caballos se arrodillan.

Sus pies cortados van, sus ojos verdes
van derramados, para siempre hundidos
en ellos los secretos y las gotas:
los túneles del mar de donde emergen,
las escaleras que el apio aconseja,
las desdichadas sombras sumergidas,
las determinaciones en el centro del aire,
los besos en el fondo de las piedras.

2. *Apogee of Celery*

From an innocent center never dinted
by sound, from the waxes' perfection,
the linear lightnings break clear:
doves with a spiral's propensities
whirled over indolent streets in an odor
of shadows and fishes.

These are the veins of the celery; the spray and the humors,
the hats of the celery!
This, the celery's signature, its firefly
taste, its cartography
soaking in colors:
its head droops, angelically green,
its delicate scallops despair;
its celery feet range the market-stalls
in the day's mutilation, sobbing:
doors close at its passing
and delectable horses kneel down.

Crop-footed, green-eyed, it flows
to all sides, and within it, the droplets,
the secret things, sunken forever:
the tunnels of ocean, whence arises
the stairway proscribed by the celery,
the disaster of shadows submerged,
the proofs in the middle of air,
the kiss in the depths of the stone.

A medianoche, con manos mojadas,
alguien golpea mi puerta en la niebla,
y oigo la voz del apio, voz profunda,
áspera voz de viento encarcelado,
se queja herido de aguas y raíces,
hunde en mi cama sus amargos rayos,
y sus desordenadas tijeras me pegan en el pecho
buscándome la boca del corazón ahogado.

Qué quieres, huésped de corsé quebradizo,
en mis habitaciones funerales?
Qué ámbito destrozado te rodea?

Fibras de oscuridad y luz llorando,
ribetes ciegos, energías crespas,
río de vida y hebras esenciales,
verdes ramas de sol acariciado,
aquí estoy, en la noche, escuchando secretos,
desvelos, soledades,
y entráis, en medio de la niebla hundida,
hasta crecer en mí, hasta comunicarme
la luz oscura y la rosa de la tierra.

At midnight, someone beats at my door
with drenched hands in the mist
and I hear a deep voice, a voice barbed
with prohibitive wind, the voice of the celery:
wounded, it rages against water and root
and plunges its bittering sheen in my bed;
the blades of its turbulent scissors strike at my breast
seeking a way to my heart under smothering water.

What would you have of me, crack-bodiced
guest in my funeral dwelling?
What ruinous ambit surrounds you?

Tissue of darkness and light and lugubrious fibers,
blind rivets, ringleted energies,
river of life, indispensable threads,
green branches beloved of the sun,
I am here, in the night, and I listen to deathwatches,
solitudes, secrets,
and you come in the midst of a lowering cloud-rack,
to root in my heart and grow great and make known to me
what is dark in the brightness, the rose of creation.

ALBERTO ROJAS JIMÉNEZ
VIENE VOLANDO

Entre plumas que asustan, entre noches,
entre magnolias, entre telegramas,
entre el viento del Sur y el Oeste marino,
    vienes volando.

Bajo las tumbas, bajo las cenizas,
bajo los caracoles congelados,
bajo las últimas aguas terrestres,
    vienes volando.

Más abajo, entre niñas sumergidas,
y plantas ciegas, y pescados rotos,
más abajo, entre nubes otra vez,
    vienes volando.

Más allá de la sangre y de los huesos,
más allá del pan, más allá del vino,
más allá del fuego,
    vienes volando.

Más allá del vinagre y de la muerte,
entre putrefacciones y violetas,
con tu celeste voz y tus zapatos húmedos,
    vienes volando.

Sobre diputaciones y farmacias,
y ruedas, y abogados, y navíos,
y dientes rojos recién arrancados,
    vienes volando.

ALBERTO ROJAS JIMÉNEZ* COMES FLYING

Between terrified feathers, between nights
and magnolias and telegrams,
between southerly winds and winds from the sea blowing
   West,
         you come flying.

Under grave-plots and ashes,
under the ice on the snail,
under the remotest terrestrial waters,
         you come flying.

Deeper still, between girls under fathoms of water,
blind plants and a litter of fish heads,
deeper, still deeper, among clouds once again
         you come flying.

Further than blood or than bones,
further than bread; beyond wines,
conflagrations,
         you come flying.

Beyond vinegar's sting and mortality,
between canker and violets,
in your heavenly voice, with the wet on your shoes,
         you come flying.

Over drugstores, committees,
over lawyers and navies, wheels
and the reddened extraction of teeth,
         you come flying.

---

*Poet, contemporary and friend of Neruda during their school years in Santiago; he met his death by drowning.

Sobre ciudades de tejado hundido
en que grandes mujeres se destrenzan
con anchas manos y peines perdidos,
	vienes volando.

Junto a bodegas donde el vino crece
con tibias manos turbias, en silencio,
con lentas manos de madera roja,
	vienes volando.

Entre aviadores desaparecidos,
al lado de canales y de sombras,
al lado de azucenas enterradas,
	vienes volando.

Entre botellas de color amargo,
entre anillos de anís y desventura,
levantando las manos y llorando,
	vienes volando.

Sobre dentistas y congregaciones,
sobre cines, y túneles y orejas,
con traje nuevo y ojos extinguidos,
	vienes volando.

Sobre tu cementerio sin paredes
donde los marineros se extravían,
mientras la lluvia de tu muerte cae,
	vienes volando.

Mientras la lluvia de tus dedos cae,
mientras la lluvia de tus huesos cae,
mientras tu médula y tu risa caen,
	vienes volando.

Over cities with roofs under water
where notable ladies uncouple the braids of their hair
with lost combs in the span of their hands
        you come flying.

Close to the ripening wine in the cellars,
with hands tepid and turbid, quiet,
with gradual, wooden, red hands
        you come flying.

Among vanishing airmen
by the banks of canals and the shadows,
beside lilies now buried,
        you come flying.

Among bitter-hued bottles,
rings of anise and accidents,
lamenting and lifting your hands,
        you come flying.

Over dentists and parishes,
cinemas, tunnels, and ears,
in your newly bought suit, with your eyeballs effaced,
        you come flying.

Over that graveyard unmarked by a wall,
where even the mariner founders,
while the rains of your death fall,
        you come flying.

While the rain of your fingertips falls,
while the rain of your bones falls,
and your laughter and marrow fall down,
        you come flying.

Sobre las piedras en que te derrites,
corriendo, invierno abajo, tiempo abajo,
mientras tu corazón desciende en gotas,
vienes volando.

No estás allí, rodeado de cemento,
y negros corazones de notarios,
y enfurecidos huesos de jinetes:
vienes volando.

Oh amapola marina, oh deudo mío,
oh guitarrero vestido de abejas,
no es verdad tanta sombra en tus cabellos:
vienes volando.

No es verdad tanta sombra persiguiéndote,
no es verdad tantas golondrinas muertas,
tanta región oscura con lamentos:
vienes volando.

El viento negro de Valparaíso
abre sus alas de carbón y espuma
para barrer el cielo donde pasas:
vienes volando.

Hay vapores, y un frío de mar muerto,
y silbatos, y meses, y un olor
de mañana lloviendo y peces sucios:
vienes volando.

Hay ron, tú y yo, y mi alma donde lloro,
y nadie, y nada, sino una escalera
de peldaños quebrados, y un paraguas:
vienes volando.

Over the flint into which you dissolve,
flowing fast under time, under winter,
while your heart falls in droplets,
           you come flying.

You are no longer there in that ring of cement,
hemmed in by the black-hearted notaries
or the horseman's maniacal bones:
           you come flying.

Oh, sea-poppy, my kinsman,
bee-clothed guitarist,
all the shadows that blacken your hair are a lie:
           you come flying.

All the shades that pursue you, a lie;
all the death-stricken swallows, a lie;
all the darkening zone of lament:
           you come flying.

A black wind from Valparaiso
spreads the charcoal and foam of its wings
to measure the sky where you pass:
           you come flying.

There are mists and the chill of dead water,
and whistles and months and the smell
of the rain in the morning and the swill of the fishes:
           you come flying.

There's rum, too, between us, you and I and the soul that
    I mourn in,
and nobody, nothing at all but a staircase
with all the treads broken, and a single umbrella:
           you come flying.

Pablo Neruda / 93

Allí está el mar. Bajo de noche y te oigo
venir volando bajo el mar sin nadie,
bajo el mar que me habita, oscurecido:
      vienes volando.

Oigo tus alas y tu lento vuelo,
y el agua de los muertos me golpea
como palomas ciegas y mojadas:
      vienes volando.

Vienes volando, solo, solitario,
solo entre muertos, para siempre solo,
vienes volando sin sombra y sin nombre,
sin azúcar, sin boca, sin rosales,
      vienes volando.

And always the sea, there. I go down in the night and I hear
    you
come flying, under water, alone,
under the sea that inhabits me, darkly:
            you come flying.

I listen for wings and your slow elevation,
while the torrents of all who have perished assail me,
blind doves flying sodden:
            you come flying.

You come flying, alone, in your solitude,
alone with the dead, alone in eternity,
shadowless, nameless, you come flying
without sweets, or a mouth, or a thicket of roses,
            you come flying.

NO HAY OLVIDO: SONATA

Si me preguntáis en dónde he estado
debo decir "Sucede".
Debo de hablar del suelo que oscurecen las piedras,
del río que durando se destruye:
no sé sino las cosas que los pájaros pierden,
el mar dejado atrás, o mi hermana llorando.
Por qué tantas regiones, por qué un día
se junta con un día? Por qué una negra noche
se acumula en la boca? Por qué muertos?

Si me preguntáis de dónde vengo, tengo que conversar
    con cosas rotas,
con utensilios demasiado amargos,
con grandes bestias a menudo podridas
y con mi acongojado corazón.

No son recuerdos los que se han cruzado
ni es la paloma amarillenta que duerme en el olvido,
sino caras con lágrimas,
dedos en la garganta,
y lo que se desploma de las hojas:
la oscuridad de un día transcurrido,
de un día alimentado con nuestra triste sangre.

He aquí violetas, golondrinas,
todo cuanto nos gusta y aparece
en las dulces tarjetas de larga cola
por donde se pasean el tiempo y la dulzura.

THERE'S NO FORGETTING (SONATA)

Ask me where have I been
and I'll tell you: "Things keep on happening."
I must talk of the rubble that darkens the stones;
of the river's duration, destroying itself;
I know only the things that the birds have abandoned,
or the ocean behind me, or my sorrowing sister.
Why the distinctions of place? Why should day
follow day? Why must the blackness
of nighttime collect in our mouths? Why the dead?

If you question me: where have you come from, I must talk
   with things falling away,
artifacts tart to the taste,
great, cankering beasts, as often as not,
and my own inconsolable heart.

Those who cross over with us, are no keepsakes,
nor the yellowing pigeon that sleeps in forgetfulness:
only the face with its tears,
the hands at our throats,
whatever the leafage dissevers:
the dark of an obsolete day,
a day that has tasted the grief in our blood.

Here are violets, swallows—
all things that delight us, the delicate tallies
that show in the lengthening train
through which pleasure and transciency pass.

Pablo Neruda / 97

Pero no penetremos más allá de esos dientes,
no mordamos las cáscaras que el silencio acumula,
porque no sé qué contestar:
hay tantos muertos,
y tantos malecones que el sol rojo partía
y tantas cabezas que golpean los buques,
y tantas manos que han encerrado besos,
y tantas cosas que quiero olvidar.

Here let us halt, in the teeth of a barrier:
useless to gnaw on the husks that the silence assembles.
For I come without answers:
see: the dying are legion,
legion, the breakwaters breached by the red of the sun,
the headpieces knocking the ship's side,
the hands closing over their kisses,
and legion the things I would give to oblivion.

LAS FURIAS Y LAS PENAS

. . . Hay en mi corazón furias y penas . . .
—Quevedo

. . . .

Tú mi enemiga de tanto sueño roto de la misma manera
que erizadas plantas de vidrio, lo mismo que campanas
deshechas de manera amenazante, tanto como disparos
de hiedra negra en medio del perfume,
enemiga de grandes caderas que mi pelo han tocado
con un ronco rocío, con una lengua de agua,
no obstante el mudo frío de los dientes y el odio de los ojos,
y la batalla de agonizantes bestias que cuidan el olvido,
en algún sitio del verano estamos juntos
acechando con labios que la sed ha invadido.

Si hay alguien que traspasa
una pared con círculos de fósforo
y hiere el centro de unos dulces miembros
y muerde cada hoja de un bosque dando gritos,
tengo también tus ojos de sangrienta luciérnaga
capaces de impregnar y atravesar rodillas
y gargantas rodeadas de seda general.

Cuando en las reuniones
el azar, la ceniza, las bebidas,
el aire interrumpido,
pero ahí están tus ojos oliendo a cacería,
a rayo verde que agujerea pechos,
tus dientes que abren manzanas de las que cae sangre,
tus piernas que se adhieren al sol dando gemidos,

. . . In my heart are the woes and the furies . . .
—QUEVEDO

. . . .

You, my antagonist, in that splintering dream
like the bristling glass of gardens, like a menace
of ruinous bells, volleys
of blackening ivy at the perfume's center,
enemy of the great hipbones my skin has touched
with a harrowing dew, with a tongue of water—
whatever the mute winter of your teeth or the hate of your
      eyes,
whatever the warfare of perishing beasts who guard our
      oblivion,
in some dominion of the summer, we are one,
ambushed with lips, in a cannonade of thirst.

If, in his phosphorous circuits,
any have entered those walls
or hewn to the center of those solacing limbs
grinding a forest foliage in his teeth, crying his pleasure,
I, too, have mastered the firefly blood of your eyes,
with its power to strike through the knees and make fruitful,
and the throats that a general silk encircles.

With the others,
the hazards, the ashes, the orgies,
the disruptions in air;
but here, your eyes reek of the hunt, a green
scintillation that bores through the bosom;
your teeth open blood in the apple,
legs crying and clasping the sun,

y tus tetas de nácar y tus pies de amapola,
como embudos llenos de dientes que buscan sombra,
como rosas hechas de látigo y perfume, y aun,
aun más, aun más,
aun detrás de los párpados, aun detrás del cielo,
aun detrás de los trajes y los viajes, en las calles donde la
    gente orina,
adivinas los cuerpos,
en las agrias iglesias a medio destruir, en las cabinas que el
    mar lleva en las manos,
acechas con tus labios sin embargo floridos,
rompes a cuchilladas la madera y la plata,
crecen tus grandes venas que asustan:
no hay cáscara, no hay distancia ni hierro,
tocan manos tus manos,
y caes haciendo crepitar las flores negras.

          . . . .

En dónde te desvistes?
En un ferrocarril, junto a un peruano rojo
o con un segador, entre terrones, a la violenta
luz del trigo?
O corres con ciertos abogados de mirada terrible
largamente desnuda, a la orilla del agua de la noche?

          . . . .

Yo persigo como en un túnel roto, en otro extremo
carne y besos que debo olvidar injustamente,
y en las aguas de espaldas, cuando ya los espejos
avivan el abismo, cuando la fatiga, los sórdidos relojes
golpean a la puerta de hoteles suburbanos, y cae
la flor de papel pintado, y de terciopelo cagado por las ratas
    y la cama

mother-of-pearl in your nipples, butterfly feet
like fangs in a funnel that grope for the darkness,
a whiplash of roses and perfume—yet more than that!
something more than that, something other,
something under your eyelids, on the other side of the sky,
something under the clothes and the voyages, the streets
    where a bypasser urinates;
you prefigure the bodies
in the bitter cathedrals halfway to ruin, in cabins the ocean
    lifts up
in its hand, you lie in your ambush, your lips no less flourish-
    ing,
you splinter the wood and the silver with dagger-thrusts,
your big veins grow great and more terrible:
distance and metal, the sheath of the pellicle
are not proof against it; hands touch your hands,
and you tumble to earth while the black petals crackle.

. . . .

Where do you loosen your clothing?
On a train, for a florid Peruvian?
Is it a harvester, under the hummocks, in the violent
    light of the wheat?
Do you race, mother-naked, with those sinister lawyers
through the watery night of the beaches?

. . . .

I follow you into that other extreme, like a wreckage of
    tunnels:
kisses and flesh I would put out of memory, wrongfully;
over watery shoulders, while the looking glass
stirs the abyss, and the niggardly clocks and the weariness
beat at the door of suburban hotels, when the nosegays
of paint-dabbled paper have fallen and rats fouled the
    velvets,

Pablo Neruda / 103

cien veces ocupada por miserables parejas, cuando
todo me dice que un día ha terminado, tú y yo
hemos estado juntos derribando cuerpos,
construyendo una casa que no dura ni muere,
tú y yo hemos corrido juntos un mismo río
con encadenadas bocas llenas de sal y sangre,
tú y yo hemos hecho temblar otra vez las luces verdes
y hemos solicitado de nuevo las grandes cenizas.

Recuerdo sólo un día
que tal vez nunca me fué destinado,
era un día incesante,
sin orígenes. Jueves.
Yo era un hombre transportado al acaso
con una mujer hallada vagamente,
nos desnudamos
como para morir o nadar o envejecer
y nos metimos uno dentro del otro,
ella rodeándome como un agujero,
yo quebrantándola como quien
golpea una campana,
pues ella era el sonido que me hería
y la cúpula dura decidida a temblar.

Era una sorda ciencia con cabello y cavernas
y machacando puntas de médula y dulzura
he rodado a las grandes coronas genitales
entre piedras y asuntos sometidos.
Este es un cuento de puertos adonde
llega uno, al azar, y sube a las colinas,
suceden tantas cosas.

when the bedstead has sagged for the woebegone couples
    a hundred
times over, and everything tells me the day has undone it-
    self—
you and I remain joined to each other, overturning the
    corpses,
building a house neither dead nor enduring,
you and I have sped down an identical river
together, mouth linked over mouth, full of blood drops and
    brine;
we have shaken the green scintillations again,
you and I, and invoked the great ashes anew.

A day never meant for me,
maybe, stays with my memory: one
whose beginning was nowhere
and endless. A Thursday.
I was that man whom hazard had joined
with a woman in uncertain encounter.
We stripped to the skin, as if
to prepare for a death or a swim, or grow old,
and forced ourselves into ourselves, one through the other.
She circled me there like a pitfall
while I stove through her flesh as a
man beats a bell;
yet she was the sound that broke open my body,
the obdurate cupola that willed its vibration.

A blind kind of science, full of caverns and hair;
I pounded the marrowy morsels and sugars
and ringed the great wreaths of her sex
between stones and surrenders.
This is a tale of the seaports
where chance brings the traveler: he clambers a hillside
and such things come to pass.

. . . .

Así es la vida,
corre tú entre las hojas, un otoño
negro ha llegado,
corre vestida con una falda de hojas y un cinturón de metal
    amarillo,
mientras la neblina de la estación roe las piedras.
Corre con tus zapatos, con tus medias,
con el gris repartido, con el hueco del pie, y con esas manos
    que el tabaco salvaje adoraría,
golpea escaleras, derriba
el papel negro que protege las puertas,
y entra en medio del sol y la ira de un día de puñales
a echarte como paloma de luto y nieve sobre un cuerpo . . .

.   .   .   .

Our whole lives were like that:
run into the leaves, a black
autumn descends,
run in your apron of leaves and a belt of gold metal
while the mist of the station house rusts on the stones.
Fly in your stockings and shoes
through the graying divisions, on the void of your feet, with
    hands that the savage tobacco might hallow,
batter the stairs and demolish
the seals that defend all the doors with black paper;
enter the pith of the sun, the rage of a day full of daggers,
and hurl yourself into your grief like a dove, like snow on the
    dead . . .

Preguntaréis: Y dónde están las lilas?
Y la metafísica cubierta de amapolas?
Y la lluvia que a menudo golpeaba
sus palabras llenándolas
de agujeros y pájaros?

Os voy a contar todo lo que me pasa.

Yo vivía en un barrio
de Madrid, con campanas,
con relojes, con árboles.

Desde allí se veía
el rostro seco de Castilla
como un océano de cuero.

                   Mi casa era llamada
la casa de las flores, porque por todas partes
estallaban geranios: era
una bella casa
con perros y chiquillos.
                Raúl, te acuerdas?
Te acuerdas, Rafael?
                Federico, te acuerdas
debajo de la tierra,
te acuerdas de mi casa con balcones en donde
la luz de junio ahogaba flores en tu boca?

         Hermano, hermano!
Todo
era grandes voces, sal de mercaderías,
aglomeraciones de pan palpitante,
mercados de mi barrio de Argüelles con su estatua

A FEW THINGS EXPLAINED

You will ask: And where are the lilacs?
And the metaphysics muffled in poppies?
And the rain which so often has battered
its words till they spouted up
gullies and birds?

I'll tell you how matters stand with me.

I lived for a time in suburban
Madrid, with its bells
and its clocks and its trees.

The face of Castile
could be seen from that place, parched,
like an ocean of leather.

        People spoke of my house
as "the house with the flowers"; it exploded
geraniums: such a beautiful
house, with the
dogs and the small fry.
        Remember, Raul?
Remember it, Rafael?
        Federico, under the ground
there, remember it?
Can you remember my house with the balconies where
June drowned the dazzle of flowers in your teeth?

        Ah, brother, my brother!
All
the voices were generous, the salt of the market place,
convocations of shimmering bread,
the stalls of suburban Argüelles with its statue

como un tintero pálido entre las merluzas:
el aceite llegaba a las cucharas,
un profundo latido
de pies y manos llenaba las calles,
metros, litros, esencia
aguda de la vida,
                    pescados hacinados,
contextura de techos con sol frío en el cual
la flecha se fatiga,
delirante marfil fino de las patatas,
tomates repetidos hasta el mar.

Y una mañana todo estaba ardiendo
y una mañana las hogueras
salían de la tierra
devorando seres,
y desde entonces fuego,
pólvora desde entonces,
y desde entonces sangre.

Bandidos con aviones y con moros,
bandidos con sortijas y duquesas,
bandidos con frailes negros bendiciendo
venían por el cielo a matar niños
y por las calles la sangre de los niños
corría simplemente, como sangre de niños.

Chacales que el chacal rechazaría,
piedras que el cardo seco mordería escupiendo,
víboras que las víboras odiarían!

Frente a vosotros he visto la sangre
de España levantarse
para ahogaros en una sola ola
de orgullo y de cuchillos!

as wan as an inkwell in the sheen of the hake:
oil swam in the spoons,
a wild pandemonium
of fingers and feet overflowing the streets,
meters and liters, all the avid
quintessence of living,
                        fish packed in the stands,
a contexture of roofs in the chill of the sun
where the arrowpoints faltered;
potatoes, inflamed and fastidious ivory,
tomatoes again and again to the sea.

Till one morning everything blazed:
one morning bonfires
sprang out of earth
and devoured all the living;
since then, only fire,
since then, the blood and the gunpowder,
ever since then.

Bandits in airplanes, Moors
and marauders with seal rings and duchesses,
black friars and brigands signed with the cross, coming
out of the clouds to a slaughter of innocents:
the blood of the children was seen in the streets,
flowing easily out, in the habit of children.

Jackals abhorred by the jackal!
Spittle of stones that the thirst of the thistle rejected,
vipers despised by the viper!

In sight of you now, I have seen
Spain uplifting its blood
in a torrent
of knives and defiance, to carry you under!

Pablo Neruda / 111

Generales
traidores:
mirad mi casa muerta,
mirad España rota:
pero de cada casa muerta sale metal ardiendo
en vez de flores,
pero de cada hueco de España
sale España,
pero de cada niño muerto sale un fusil con ojos,
pero de cada crimen nacen balas
que os hallarán un día el sitio
del corazón.

Preguntaréis por qué su poesía
no nos habla del suelo, de las hojas,
de los grandes volcanes de su país natal?

Venid a ver la sangre por las calles,
venid a ver
la sangre por las calles,
venid a ver la sangre
por las calles!

Turncoats
and generals:
see the death of my house,
look well at the havoc of Spain:
out of dead houses it is metal that blazes
in place of the flowers,
out of the ditches of Spain
it is Spain that emerges,
out of the murder of children, a gunsight with eyes,
out of your turpitude, bullets are born
that one day will strike for the mark
of your hearts.

Would you know why his poems
never mention the soil or the leaves,
the gigantic volcanoes of the country that bore him?

Come see the blood in the streets,
come see
the blood in the streets,
come see the blood
in the streets!

CÓMO ERA ESPAÑA

Era España tirante y seca, diurno
tambor de són opaco,
llanura y nido de águilas, silencio
de azotada intemperie.

Cómo, hasta el llanto, hasta el alma
amo tu duro suelo, tu pan pobre,
tu pueblo pobre, cómo hasta el hondo sitio
de mi ser hay la flor perdida de tus aldeas
arrugadas, inmóviles de tiempo,
y tus campiñas minerales
extendidas en luna y en edad
y devoradas por un dios vacío.

Todas tus estructuras, tu animal
aislamiento junto a tu inteligencia
rodeada por las piedras abstractas del silencio,
tu áspero vino, tu suave
vino, tus violentas
y delicadas viñas.

Piedra solar, pura entre las regiones
del mundo, España recorrida
por sangres y metales, azul y victoriosa
proletaria de pétalos y balas, única
viva y soñolienta y sonora.

HOW SPAIN WAS

Arid and taut—day's drumskin,
a sounding opacity: that's how Spain was:
an eyrie for eagles, flat-landed, a silence
under the thong of the weathers.

How, with my soul and my tears,
I have cherished your obstinate soil, your destitute bread
and your peoples; how, in the deepest
recess of my being, the flower of your villages,
furrowed, immobile in time, lives for me, lost,
with your flinty savannas
magnified under the moon and the eons,
gorged by a fatuous god.

All your animal
loneliness, joined to your judgment, all things built with
    your hands
in a compass of silence bounded abstractly by stones,
your vintages, the suave
and the coarse, your aroused
and your delicate vines.

Great sunstone, unflawed in the zones
of the world, Spain threaded
by bloods and by metals, triumphant and blue,
proletariat of petals and bullets whom nothing repeats in
    the world:
sonorous, comatose, living.

Pablo Neruda / 115

Canto General / General Song
(1950)

ALGUNAS BESTIAS

Era el crepúsculo de la iguana.

Desde la arcoirisada crestería
su lengua como un dardo
se hundía en la verdura,
el hormiguero monacal pisaba
con melodioso pie la selva,
el guanaco fino como el oxígeno
en las anchas alturas pardas
iba calzando botas de oro,
mientras la llama abría cándidos
ojos en la delicadeza
del mundo lleno de rocío.

Los monos trenzaban un hilo
interminablemente erótico
en las riberas de la aurora,
derribando muros de polen
y espantando el vuelo violeta
de las mariposas de Muzo.

Era la noche de los caimanes,
la noche pura y pululante
de hocicos saliendo del légamo,
y de las ciénagas soñolientas
un ruido opaco de armaduras
volvía al origen terrestre.

SOME BEASTS

It was the twilight of the iguana:

From a rainbowing battlement,
a tongue like a javelin
lunging in verdure;
an ant heap treading the jungle,
monastic, on musical feet;
the guanaco, oxygen-fine
in the high places swarthy with distances,
cobbling his feet into gold;
the llama of scrupulous eye
that widens his gaze on the dews
of a delicate world.

A monkey is weaving
a thread of insatiable lusts
on the margins of morning:
he topples a pollen-fall,
startles the violet flight
of the butterfly, wings on the Muzo.

It was the night of the alligator:
snouts moving out of the slime,
in original darkness, pullulations,
a clatter of armor, opaque
in the sleep of the bog,
turning back to the chalk of the sources.

El jaguar tocaba las hojas
con su ausencia fosforescente,
el puma corre en el ramaje
como el fuego devorador
mientras arden en él los ojos
alcohólicos de la selva.
Los tejones rascan los pies
del río, husmean el nido
cuya delicia palpitante
atacarán con dientes rojos.

Y en el fondo del agua magna,
como el círculo de la tierra,
está la gigante anaconda
cubierta de barros rituales,
devoradora y religiosa.

The jaguar touches the leaves
with his phosphorous absence,
the puma speeds through the branches
in the blaze of his hungers,
his eyeballs, a jungle of alcohol,
burn in his head.
Badgers are raking the river beds,
nuzzling the havens
for their warm delectation,
red-toothed, for assault.

And below, on the vastness of water,
like a continent circled,
drenched in the ritual mud,
rapacious, religious,
gigantic, the coiled anaconda.

IV

La poderosa muerte me invitó muchas veces:
era como la sal invisible en las olas,
y lo que su invisible sabor diseminaba
era como mitades de hundimientos y altura
o vastas construcciones de viento y ventisquero.

Yo al férreo filo vine, a la angostura
del aire, a la mortaja de agricultura y piedra,
al estelar vacío de los pasos finales
y a la vertiginosa carretera espiral:
pero, ancho mar, oh, muerte!, de ola en ola no vienes,
sino como un galope de claridad nocturna
o como los totales números de la noche.

Nunca llegaste a hurgar en el bolsillo, no era
posible tu visita sin vestimenta roja:
sin auroral alfombra de cercado silencio:
sin altos o enterrados patrimonios de lágrimas.

No pude amar en cada ser un árbol
con su pequeño otoño a cuestas (la muerte de mil hojas),
todas las falsas muertes y las resurrecciones
sin tierra, sin abismo:
quise nadar en las más anchas vidas,
en las más sueltas desembocaduras,
y cuando poco a poco el hombre fué negándome
y fué cerrando paso y puerta para que no tocaran
mis manos manantiales su inexistencia herida,
entonces fuí por calle y calle y río y río,

Death, overmastering all, has beckoned me often:
eye has not seen it, like brine in the wave,
but invisible savors are shed on the waters,
height, or the ruin of height, a plenitude halved,
enormous constructions of ice and the wind.

I had come to the limits of iron, a narrowing
air, to the graveclothes of gardens and stones,
vacancy starred with the tread of the ultimate,
and the dizzying whorl of the highway:
but not with a billow's successions you come to us, Death!
though the sea of our dying is ample, you strike at a gallop,
explicit in darkness, and the numbers of midnight are reck-
   oned.

No pickpocket rifler, you come to us; lacking
that scarlet investiture, no advent is possible:
you tread on the weft of the morning, enclosing a quietness,
a heritage weeping above us, tears underground.

That tree of our being,
with its nondescript autumns (a thousand leaves dying),
that fardel of fraudulent deaths, resurrections
out of nowhere—neither earth, nor abysses of earth:
I never could cherish it.
I prayed to the drench of life's amplitude, a swimmer,
unencumbered, at the place of the sources;
until, little by little, denied by the others—those
who would seal up their doors and their footfalls and with-
   hold
their wounded non-being from the gush of my fingers—
I came by another way, river by river, street after street,

y ciudad y ciudad y cama y cama,
y atravesó el desierto mi máscara salobre,
y en las últimas casas humilladas, sin lámpara, sin fuego,
sin pan, sin piedra, sin silencio, solo,
rodé muriendo de mi propia muerte.

V

No eres tú, muerte grave, ave de plumas férreas,
la que el pobre heredero de las habitaciones
llevaba entre alimentos apresurados, bajo la piel vacía:
era algo, un pobre pétalo de cuerda exterminada:
un átomo del pecho que no vino al combate
o el áspero rocío que no cayó en la frente.
Era lo que no pudo renacer, un pedazo
de la pequeña muerte sin paz ni territorio:
un hueso, una campana que morían en él.
Yo levanté las vendas del yodo, hundí las manos
en los pobres dolores que mataban la muerte,
y no encontré en la herida sino una racha fría
que entraba por los vagos intersticios del alma.

VII

Muertos de un solo abismo, sombras de una
      hondonada,
la profunda, es así como al tamaño
de vuestra magnitud
vino la verdadera, la más abrasadora
muerte y desde las rocas taladradas,
desde los capiteles escarlata,
desde los acueductos escalares
os desplomasteis como en un otoño
en una sola muerte.
Hoy el aire vacío ya no llora,

city by city, one bed and another,
forcing the salt of my mask through a wilderness;
and there, in the shame of the ultimate hovels, lampless and
    fireless,
lacking bread or a stone or a stillness, alone in myself,
I whirled at my will, dying the death that was mine.

V

Not feathered with iron, portentous in dying—not that way
the impoverished spawn of the hamlet inherit you, Death:
they wear in the void of their skins a more urgent subsistence,
a thing of their own, poor petal, a raveling cord,
the mote in the bosom that never confronted its quarrel,
the forehead's arduous sweat drop that never was given.
Theirs is the little death, placeless and respiteless,
a morsel of dying no second renewal could quicken:
a bone or a perishing bell-sound razed from within.
I opened a bandage of iodine, steeping my hands
in the starveling despairs that would murder their dying,
but nothing declared itself there in the wound, nothing
    came forth:
only spaces of spirit where vaguely the bitter chill blew.

VII

O you dead of a common abysm, shades of a chasm,
see where the depths lead! it is this way: as if
to your magnitude's measure,
death's perfectness came in the quick of a holocaust;
as if, from the ravage
of drillers, the crimson pilasters
and staggered ascents of the aqueducts,
you veered out of plumb, indivisibly
dying, and crashed like an autumn.
The hollow of air will lament you no longer,

Pablo Neruda / 125

ya no conoce vuestros pies de arcilla,
ya olvidó vuestros cántaros que filtraban el cielo
cuando lo derramaban los cuchillos del rayo,
y el árbol poderoso fué comido
por la niebla, y cortado por la racha.
Él sostuvo una mano que cayó de repente
desde la altura hasta el final del tiempo.
Ya no sois, manos de araña, débiles
hebras, tela enmarañada:
cuanto fuistes cayó: costumbres, sílabas
raídas, máscaras de luz deslumbradora.

Pero una permanencia de piedra y de palabra:
la ciudad como un vaso se levantó en las manos
de todos, vivos, muertos, callados, sostenidos
de tanta muerte, un muro, de tanta vida un golpe
de pétalos de piedra: la rosa permanente, la morada:
este arrecife andino de colonias glaciales.

Cuando la mano de color de arcilla
se convirtió en arcilla, y cuando los pequeños párpados se
    cerraron
llenos de ásperos muros, poblados de castillos,
y cuando todo el hombre se enredó en su agujero,
quedó la exactitud enarbolada:
el alto sitio de la aurora humana:
la más alta vasija que contuvo el silencio:
una vida de piedra después de tantas vidas.

nor acknowledge the chalk of your footfalls;
your cruses that filtered the sky
brimming the light with a sunburst of knives,
are forgotten; the power that lives in the tree
is devoured by the haze and struck down by the wind.
Suddenly, out of the summits, into uttermost time,
the hand that it cradled has toppled.
All that spidery finger-play, the gimcrack
device of the fibers, the meshes' entanglements—you have
    put them behind.
All that you were, falls away: habitudes, tatterdemalion
syllables, the blinding personae of light.

We come upon permanence: the rock that abides and the
    word:
the city upraised like a cup in our fingers,
all hands together, the quick and the dead and the quiet-
    ened; death's
plenitude holding us here, a bastion, the fullness
of life like a blow falling, petals of flint
and the perduring rose, abodes for the sojourner.
a glacier for multitudes, breakwater in Andes.

Now when the clay-colored hand is made
one with the clay, diminutive eyelids close over,
crammed with the bruise of the walls, peopled with castles,
as if our humanity tangled itself in a bog—
a leafy exactitude stays:
the high places, holding our human beginnings:
that steepest alembic encircling our silence:
life like an adamant, after the fleeting of lives.

DUERME UN SOLDADO

Extraviado en los límites espesos
llegó el soldado. Era total fatiga
y cayó entre las lianas y las hojas,
al pie del Gran Dios emplumado:
éste
estaba solo con su mundo apenas
surgido de la selva.
                Miró al soldado
extraño nacido del océano.
Miró sus ojos, su barba sangrienta,
su espada, el brillo negro
de la armadura, el cansancio caído
como la bruma sobre esa cabeza
de niño carnicero.
Cuántas zonas
de oscuridad para que el Dios de Pluma
naciera y enroscara su volumen
sobre los bosques, en la piedra rosada,
cuánto desorden de aguas locas
y de noche salvaje, el desbordado
cauce de la luz sin nacer, el fermento rabioso
de las vidas, la destrucción, la harina
de la fertilidad y luego el orden,
el orden de la planta y de la secta,
la elevación de las rocas cortadas,
el humo de las lámparas rituales,
la firmeza del suelo para el hombre,
el establecimiento de las tribus,
el tribunal de los dioses terrestres.

SOLDIER ASLEEP

Derelict there in the leafy encirclement,
the soldier arrived. His weariness struck at him then,
and he fell in the leaves and lianas
at the foot of that Providence, the plumed and omnipotent
God
alone with His universe, still
warm from the jungles.
                        Godhead looked long
at the warrior outlandishly born from the sea water:
stared long at those eyes, at the blood-clabbered beard
and the sword, the black scintillation
of armor, the weariness weighing
like haze on the head
of the bloody young man.
How many zones
in the darkness, till the God of the Feathers
could be born and entwine on the wood
and the roseate stone, the web of his volume!
What a chaos of lunatic water,
nocturnal ferocity, what ravening
troughs for the light, unregenerate yet, what
crazed fermentation of lives and destructions, what bran
of fertility, before the decorum could come:
the orders of plants and of clans,
the cut stone disposed on the stone,
the smoke of the ritual lamps,
soil firm for the stance of a man,
disposition of tribes
and tribunes of terrestrial gods!

Palpitó cada escama de la piedra,
sintió el pavor caído
como una invasión de insectos,
recogió todo su poderío,
hizo llegar la lluvia a las raíces,
habló con las corrientes de la tierra,
oscuro en su vestido
de piedra cósmica inmovilizada,
y no pudo mover garras ni dientes,
ni ríos, ni temblores,
ni meteoros que silbaran
en la bóveda del reinado,

y quedó allí, piedra inmóvil, silencio,

mientras Beltrán de Córdoba dormía.

All the flakes of the rock shook:
it felt the descent of the Terror
like a swarming of insects,
and massing the might of its properties,
sent rain to the roots,
conferred with the motions of earth
still unmoved and obscure in the stone
of its cosmic investiture,
unable to stir in a fang or a claw,
a river, a temblor,
a meteor's hiss
through the pit of its emperies:

and remained in that place, like a silence, a stone immo-
    bility,

while Beltrán of Córdoba slept on.

De dónde soy, me pregunto a veces, de dónde diablos
vengo, qué día es hoy, qué pasa,
ronco, en medio del sueño, del árbol, de la noche,
y una ola se levanta como un párpado, un día
nace de ella, un relámpago con hocico de tigre.

Despierto de pronto en la noche pensando
en el Extremo Sur . . .

Viene el día y me dice: "Oyes
el agua lenta, el agua,
el agua,
sobre la Patagonia?"
Y yo contesto: "Sí, señor, escucho."
Viene el día y me dice: "Una oveja salvaje
lejos, en la región, lame el color helado
de una piedra. No escuchas el balido, no reconoces
el vendaval azul en cuyas manos
la luna es una copa, no ves la tropa, el dedo
rencoroso del viento
tocar la ola y la vida con su anillo vacío?"

Recuerdo la soledad
del estrecho.

La larga noche, el pino, vienen adonde voy.
Y se trastorna el ácido sordo, la fatiga,
la tapa del tonel, cuanto tengo en la vida.
Una gota de nieve llora y llora en mi puerta
mostrando su vestido claro y desvencijado
de pequeño cometa que me busca y solloza.

Where am I from, I ask myself, where the devil
am I from, what's today, what goes on
here, in the midst of the dream and the tree and the night—
    huskily—
and a wave rises up like an eyelid, and a day
rises out of it, a flash like the snout of a tiger.

And suddenly wake up in the night
and think of that Far South . . .

Day comes and tells me: Don't you hear it?
The water, the water,
slow water,
Patagonian water?
And I answer: Sure, mister, I hear it.
Day comes and says to me: Far off
there's a place where the cattle run wild, the sheep
lap the cold coloration
of stone. Don't you hear all that bawling, remember
the hurricane blue of those fingers
that circle the moon like a cup, don't you see the stampede,
the malevolent fingers of wind
touching the wave, touching our lives like the void in a ring?

I remember my loneliness
there in that Strait.

The long night and the pine are with me wherever I go.
The barrel bung topples
its stupefied acids, weariness, the lees of my lifetime.
Snow blubbers and whines at my door, a drop at a time,
looking limpid and frayed, like a comet in clothing,
a little one, whimpering, searching me out.

Nadie mira la ráfaga, la extensión, el aullido
del aire en las praderas.

Me acerco y digo: vamos. Toco el Sur, desemboco
en la arena, veo la planta seca y negra, todo raíz
    y roca,
las islas arañadas por el agua y el cielo,
el Río del Hambre, el Corazón de Ceniza,
el Patio del Mar Lúgubre, y donde silba
la solitaria serpiente, donde cava
el último zorro herido y esconde su tesoro sangriento
encuentro la tempestad y su voz de ruptura,
su voz de viejo libro, su boca de cien labios,
algo me dice, algo que el aire devora cada día.

Los descubridores aparecen
y de ellos no queda nada.

Recuerda el agua cuanto le sucedió al navío.
La dura tierra extraña guarda sus calaveras
que suenan en el pánico austral como cornetas
y ojos de hombre y de buey dan al día su hueco,
su anillo, su sonido de implacable estelaje.
El viejo cielo busca la vela,
                              nadie
ya sobrevive: el buque destruído
vive con la ceniza del marinero amargo,
y de los puestos de oro, de las casas de cuero
del trigo pestilente, y de
la llama fría de las navegaciones
(cuánto golpe en la noche [roca y bajel] al fondo)

No one stands to the squall on the stormy expanse, the how-
    ling
of air in those meadows.

I go up to them then and I say: let's get going. Somewhere
    South, we touch land,
put in on a sandbar; I see black vegetation, bone-dry,
    boulder and bracken, all of it,
islands clawed by the water and sky:
the River-Called-Hunger, the Court
of the Woebegone Waters, Cinder-Heart—and there
where a lone serpent hisses, the last of the foxes
caches his blood-spattered treasury,
digging in bloodily, I tack toward a hurricane, a sound of
    things breaking,
that old book of a voice, a hundred lips talking as one, a
    mouth
telling me something, something undone in thin air.

The discoverers come;
nothing is left of them now.

Whatever took hold of our ship is remembered by water.
An alien and obdurate earth holds their skulls—
a noise of cornets in a panic equator.
Eyeballs of oxen and men turn their void to the day, turn
their finger-rings up, the implacable sound of the wake.
The old sky is searching the sails;
                                but no one
survived it: the shipwreck
remains and the ash of the truculent sailor;
from the gilded encampments and the leathery compounds
of wheat, pestilential, from the
cold fire of voyage
(what shocks from the depths in the night—vessel and rock!)

Pablo Neruda / 135

sólo queda el dominio quemado y sin cadáveres,
la incesante intemperie apenas rota
por un negro fragmento
de fuego fallecido.

Sólo se impone
la desolación.

Esfera que destroza lentamente la noche, el agua, el hielo,
extensión combatida por el tiempo y el término,
con su marca violeta, con el final azul
del arco iris salvaje
se sumergen los pies de mi patria en tu sombra
y aúlla y agoniza la rosa triturada.

Recuerdo al
viejo descubridor.

Por el canal navega nuevamente
el cereal helado, la barba del combate,
el Otoño glacial, el transitorio herido.
Con él, con el antiguo, con el muerto,
con el destituído por el agua rabiosa,
con él, en su tormenta, con su frente.

Aún lo sigue el albatros y la soga de cuero
comida, con los ojos fuera de la mirada
y el ratón devorado ciegamente mirando
entre los palos rotos el esplendor iracundo,
mientras en el vacío la sortija y el hueso
caen, resbalan sobre la vaca marina.

only the burning dominion lives on, without corpses,
the unwearying work of the weather, barely scarred
by a black fragmentation
of flares gutting out.

Only havoc
stands firm.

A globe working piecemeal on water and ice and the night,
    a destroyer,
vastitude stricken by time and finality
in its violet signature, the ultimate blues
of a turbulent rainbow:
the keel of my country is drowned in your shadow
and the smashed rose howls in a death agony.

I call up
the olden discoverer.

Once more in the channel ways
a frozen provender sails, the beards with the battle-blows,
the wounds of the casuals, the glacial autumns.
They go with him there, with his death, with the old one,
him whom the ravening waters abandoned,
go on with him into his torment, into his thoughts.

Even the albatross follows and the rust
of the leathery cable—eyes probing the visible—
the starved rat blindly gazing
at angry magnificence through a rubble of spars
where finger-rings fall through the emptiness, bones
slip away on the cow of old ocean.

Magallanes.

Cuál es el dios que pasa? Mirad su barba llena de gusanos
y sus calzones en que la espesa atmósfera
se pega y muerde como un perro náufrago:
y tiene peso de ancla maldita su estatura,
y silba el piélago y el aquilón acude
hasta sus pies mojados.
                              Caracol de la oscura
sombra del tiempo,
                              espuela
carcomida, viejo señor de luto litoral, aguilero
sin estirpe, manchado manantial, el estiércol
del Estrecho te manda,
y no tiene de cruz tu pecho sino un grito
del mar, un grito blanco, de luz marina,
y de tenaza, de tumbo en tumbo, de aguijón demolido.

Llega al Pacífico.

Porque el siniestro día del mar termina un día,
y la mano nocturna corta uno a uno sus dedos
hasta no ser, hasta que el hombre nace
y el capitán descubre dentro de sí el acero
y la América sube su burbuja
y la costa levanta su pálido arrecife
sucio de aurora, turbio de nacimiento
hasta que de la nave sale un grito y se ahoga
y otro grito y el alba que nace de la espuma.

Magellan

What god comes this way? Look at the worm-eaten
beard, the knee breeches bitten and soaked
in the thickening air, old dog in a shipwreck:
his stature already bears down with the weight of an anchor
    accursed,
the sea lanes at flood whistle by, a north wind attends him
wetting his feet at its verge.
                    Sea shell
in the shadowy backward of time,
                          mouldering
spur, patriarch coastland lamenting, eyrie
unpedigreed, headwater fouled—the dung
of the Narrows commands you;
except for a cry from the depths, your breast is unmarked
by a cross, the white of a scream, a watery flash
and a claw, a whiplash subsiding, somersaults, heels over
    bum.

He sees the Pacific.

Because the sinister sea-day shall one day come to an end
and the night of the hand cut its fingers away,
finger for finger, till nothing remains and man is reborn:
because the Captain discovers within himself, steel,
and America lifts up its bubble,
the coastlands heave to, in a pallor of reefs,
birth-sodden, clotted with dawn,
and the ship's cry is heard in the hold, and goes under,
and another cry comes and morning is born from the foam.

Todos han muerto.

Hermanos de agua y piojo, de planeta carnívoro:
visteis, al fin, el árbol del mástil agachado
por la tormenta? Visteis la piedra machacada
bajo la loca nieve brusca de la ráfaga?
Al fin, ya tenéis vuestro paraíso perdido,
al fin, tenéis vuestra guarnición maldiciente,
al fin, vuestros fantasmas atravesados del aire
besan sobre la arena la huella de la foca.
Al fin, a vuestros dedos sin sortija
llega el pequeño sol del páramo, el día muerto,
temblando, en su hospital de olas y piedras.

All of them dead.

Brothers of vermin and ocean, a carnivorous planet,
do you see, in the end, how the mast tree is bowed
by the storm? Do you see the detritus of stone
under lunatic snow, like a bolt from the squall?
A paradise lost is yours again now
in the end; the garrison mouthing its curses is yours
in the end; your phantoms transfixed in the air
kiss the tracks of the seal in the sand, in the end.
In the end, to your ring fingers, naked of rings,
comes the sun of the uplands, still very small, the dead day
atremble, in its hospice of wavelets and stones.

Qué hicisteis vosotros gidistas,
intelectualistas, rilkistas,
misterizantes, falsos brujos
existenciales, amapolas
surrealistas encendidas
en una tumba, europeizados
cadáveres de la moda,
pálidas lombrices del queso
capitalista, qué hicisteis
ante el reinado de la angustia,
frente a este oscuro ser humano,
a esta pateada compostura,
a esta cabeza sumergida
en el estiércol, a esta esencia
de ásperas vidas pisoteadas?

No hicisteis nada sino la fuga:
vendisteis hacinado detritus,
buscasteis cabellos celestes,
plantas cobardes, uñas rotas,
"Belleza pura," "sortilegio,"
obra de pobres asustados
para evadir los ojos, para
enmarañar las delicadas
pupilas, para subsistir
con el plato de restos sucios
que os arrojaron los señores,
sin ver la piedra en agonía,
sin defender, sin conquistar,
más ciegos que las coronas
del cementerio, cuando cae
la lluvia sobre las inmóviles
flores podridas de las tumbas.

POETS CELESTIAL

What has it come to, you Gideans,
Rilkeans, intellect-mongers,
obscurantists, false
existential witch doctors, surrealist
butterflies ablaze
on the carrion, you up-to-the-minute
continental cadavers,
green grubs in the cheeses
of Capital—what did you do
in the kingdoms of agony,
in sight of a nameless humanity
and their vexed acquiescence,
heads drowned
in the offal, the harrowed
quintessence of life trampled under?

Flight and escape: nothing more. You peddled
the rinds of the midden-heap,
probed for a heaven of hair,
pusillanimous plants, fingernail parings:
"pure Beauty," "sorcery"—
all that wretched device of the fainthearted
averting their gazes, looking askance,
disengaging their delicate
eyeballs, to root in a
platter of rinsings and garbage
flung down to you there by the lordlings,
blind to the agon that works in the stone,
disclaiming all quarrels, undefended:
blinder by far than the funeral
wreath in the rain of the graveyard,
that falls on the motionless
compost of flowers, on the mounds.

Pablo Neruda | 143

Eran muchos, llevaban el ídolo
sobre los hombros, era espesa
la cola de la muchedumbre
como una salida del mar
con morada fosforescencia.

Saltaban bailando, elevando
graves murmullos masticados
que se unían a la fritanga
y a los tétricos tamboriles.

Chalecos morados, zapatos
morados, sombreros
llenaban de manchas violetas
las avenidas como un río
de enfermendades pustulosas
que desembocaba en los vidrios
inútiles de la catedral.
Algo infinitamente lúgubre
como el incienso, la copiosa
aglomeración de las llagas
hería los ojos uniéndose
con las llamas afrodisíacas
del apretado río humano.

Vi al obeso terrateniente
sudando en los sobrepellices,
rascándose los goterones
de sagrada esperma en la nuca.

PROCESSION IN LIMA: 1947

There were many to shoulder
the idol: multitudes
packed into queues and
debouching like sea water
phosphorescent with purple.

Dancing and leaping and grinding
their teeth on a ritual mumble,
in a merging of voices: fish-fry and chicken-gut
and dour tambourines.

Lavender waistcoats and lavender
shoes, hats smutty
with violet,
avenues brimming like rivers
with the sick and the pustulant
that emptied their filth
on the impotent glass of cathedrals.
A thing inexhaustibly
sad, like the incense, an extravagant
rabble of ulcers
wounding the onlooker, that merged
with the aphrodisiacal fire
and fused in a sea of the living.

I looked long: at the swag-bellied
landholders, sweaty with surplices,
scratching the droplets
of hallowing sperm from their neckbands.

Pablo Neruda / 145

Vi al zaparrastroso gusano
de las estériles montañas,
al indio de rostro perdido
en las vasijas, al pastor
de llamas dulces, a las niñas
cortantes de las sacristías,
a los profesores de aldea
con rostros azules y hambrientos.
Narcotizados bailadores
con camisones purpurinos
iban los negros pataleando
sobre tambores invisibles.
Y todo el Perú se golpeaba
el pecho mirando la estatua
de una señora remilgada,
azul-celeste y rosadilla
que navegaba las cabezas
en su barco de confitura
hinchado de aire sudoroso.

Saw the slovenly worm
in the mountain's sterility,
the Indian faces supine among platters
and cannikins; mild llamas
and llama-boys; the gaunt
virgins that languish in sacristies,
parochial schoolmasters
blue-faced and hunger-marked.
Narcotic with dancing,
stamping their feet on invisible
drums, the negroes moved on
in their amethyst nightgowns.
A country was beating its breastbone—
the whole of Peru, with its gaze
on an idol, sky-blue and roseate,
our lady of niceties
parting their heads like a sea
in her shallop of sugar-stick
and swelling a sweltering air.

LA UNITED FRUIT CO.

Cuando sonó la trompeta, estuvo
todo preparado en la tierra,
y Jehová repartió el mundo
a Coca-Cola Inc., Anaconda,
Ford Motors, y otras entidades:
la Compañía Frutera Inc.
se reservó lo más jugoso,
la costa central de mi tierra,
la dulce cintura de América.
Bautizó de nuevo sus tierras
como "Repúblicas Bananas,"
y sobre los muertos dormidos,
sobre los héroes inquietos
que conquistaron la grandeza,
la libertad y las banderas,
estableció la ópera bufa:
enajenó los albedríos,
regaló coronas de César,
desenvainó la envidia, atrajo
la dictadura de las moscas,
moscas Trujillos, moscas Tachos,
moscas Carías, moscas Martínez,
moscas Ubico, moscas húmedas
de sangre humilde y mermelada,
moscas borrachas que zumban
sobre las tumbas populares,
moscas de circo, sabias moscas
entendidas en tiranía.

THE UNITED FRUIT CO.

When the trumpets had sounded and all
was in readiness on the face of the earth,
Jehovah divided his universe:
Anaconda, Ford Motors,
Coca-Cola Inc., and similar entities:
the most succulent item of all,
The United Fruit Company Incorporated
reserved for itself: the heartland
and coasts of my country,
the delectable waist of America.
They rechristened their properties:
the "Banana Republics"—
and over the languishing dead,
the uneasy repose of the heroes
who harried that greatness,
their flags and their freedoms,
they established an *opéra bouffe:*
they ravished all enterprise,
awarded the laurels like Caesars,
unleashed all the covetous, and contrived
the tyrannical Reign of the Flies—
Trujillo the fly, and Tacho the fly,
the flies called Carias, Martinez,
Ubico—all of them flies, flies
dank with the blood of their marmalade
vassalage, flies buzzing drunkenly
on the populous middens:
the fly-circus fly and the scholarly
kind, case-hardened in tyranny.

Entre las moscas sanguinarias
la Frutera desembarca,
arrasando el café y las frutas,
en sus barcos que deslizaron
como bandejas el tesoro
de nuestras tierras sumergidas.

Mientras tanto, por los abismos
azucarados de los puertos,
caían indios sepultados
en el vapor de la mañana:
un cuerpo rueda, una cosa
sin nombre, un número caído,
un racimo de fruta muerta
derramada en el pudridero.

Then in the bloody domain of the flies
The United Fruit Company Incorporated
unloaded with a booty of coffee and fruits
brimming its cargo boats, gliding
like trays with the spoils
of our drowning dominions.

And all the while, somewhere, in the sugary
hells of our seaports,
smothered by gases, an Indian
fell in the morning:
a body spun off, an anonymous
chattel, some numeral tumbling,
a branch with its death running out of it
in the vat of the carrion, fruit laden and foul.

LOS MENDIGOS

Junto a las catedrales, anudados
al muro, acarrearon
sus pies, sus bultos, sus miradas negras,
sus crecimientos lívidos de gárgolas,
sus latas andrajosas de comida,
y desde allí, desde la dura
santidad de la piedra,
se hicieron flora de la calle, errantes
flores de las legales pestilencias.

El parque tiene sus mendigos
como sus árboles de torturados
ramajes y raíces:
a los pies del jardín vive el esclavo,
como al final del hombre, hecho basura,
aceptada su impura simetría,
listo para la escoba de la muerte.

La caridad lo entierra
en su agujero de tierra leprosa:
sirve de ejemplo al hombre de mis días.
Debe aprender a pisotear, a hundir
la especie en los pantanos del desprecio,
a poner los zapatos en la frente
del ser con uniforme de vencido,
o por lo menos debe comprenderlo
en los productos de la naturaleza.
Mendigo americano, hijo del año
1948, nieto
de catedrales, yo no te venero,
yo no voy a poner marfil antiguo,
barbas de rey en tu escrita figura,
como te justifican en los libros,

THE BEGGARS

By the cathedrals, clotting
the walls, they deploy
with their bundles, their black looks, their limbs,
ripped tins of provender,
the livid increase of the gargoyles;
beyond, on the obdurate
unction of stone
they nurture a gutter-flower, the flower
of legitimized plague, in migrations.

The park has its paupers
like its trees of extortionate
foliage and root-forms:
at the garden's margin, the slave,
like a sink at the verge of humanity,
content with his tainted dissymmetry
supine by the broom of his dying.

Though charity bury them
in the pit of their pestilence,
they suffice for the human condition: they prefigure us.
Our wisdom is this: to trample them under,
to harry the breed in the sties of contempt,
servility's creatures, wearing servility's livery—
we may show them our bootsoles
or interpret their lack in the order of nature.
American panhandlers, '48's
offspring, grandsons
of church doors, I do not commend you.
I will not invest you with ivory usages,
the rhetorists' figure, monarchical beards,
or explain you away with a book, like the others.

Pablo Neruda / 153

yo te voy a borrar con esperanza:
no entrarás a mi amor organizado,
no entrarás a mi pecho con los tuyos,
con los que te crearon escupiendo
tu forma degradada,
yo apartaré tu arcilla de la tierra
hasta que te construyan los metales
y salgas a brillar como una espada.

I efface you, and hope—
who never will enter my discipline's love,
neither you nor your pieties, nor pass to my pity.
I exile your dust from the earth
and those who contrived you to soil
a contemptible image—
till metals remake you
and you issue and blaze like a blade.

UN ASESINO DUERME

La cintura manchada por el vino
cuando el dios tabernario
pisa los vasos rotos y desgreña
la luz del alba desencadenada:
la rosa humedecida en el sollozo
de la pequeña prostituta, el viento de los días febriles
que entra por la ventana sin cristales
donde el vengado duerme con los zapatos puestos
en un olor amargo de pistolas,
en un color azul de ojos perdidos.

SLEEPING ASSASSIN

A wine-spotted waist
for the tavern-god
treading the wreckage of glasses, disheveling
dawn's glowing divisions—
a moistening rose in the prostitute's whimper,
where the wind spends the fevers of morning
in a windowpane's void,
and the gunman, still booted for vengeance,
in a sour exhalation of pistols,
and a blue-eyed disaster, sleeps sound.

JUVENTUD

Un perfume como una ácida espada
de ciruelas en un camino,
los besos del azúcar en los dientes,
las gotas vitales resbalando en los dedos,
la dulce pulpa erótica,
las eras, los pajares, los incitantes
sitios secretos de las casas anchas,
los colchones dormidos en el pasado, el agrio valle verde
mirado desde arriba, desde el vidrio escondido:
toda la adolescencia mojándose y ardiendo
como una lámpara derribada en la lluvia.

YOUTH

Acid and sword blade: the fragrance
of plum in the pathways:
tooth's sweetmeat of kisses,
power and spilth on the fingers,
the yielding erotic of pulps,
hayricks and threshing floors, clandestine
recesses that tempt through the vastness of houses;
bolsters asleep in the past, the bitter green valley,
seen from above, from the glasses' concealment;
and drenching and flaring by turns, adolescence
like a lamp overturned in the rain.

LOS DICTADORES

Ha quedado un olor entre los cañaverales:
una mezcla de sangre y cuerpo, un penetrante
pétalo nauseabundo.
Entre los cocoteros las tumbas están llenas
de huesos demolidos, de estertores callados.
El delicado sátrapa conversa
con copas, cuellos y cordones de oro.
El pequeño palacio brilla como un reloj
y las rápidas risas enguantadas
atraviesan a veces los pasillos
y se reúnen a las voces muertas
y a las bocas azules frescamente enterradas.
El llanto está escondido como una planta
cuya semilla cae sin cesar sobre el suelo
y hace crecer sin luz sus grandes hojas ciegas.
El odio se ha formado escama a escama,
golpe a golpe, en el agua terrible del pantano,
con un hocico lleno de légamo y silencio.

THE DICTATORS

An odor stayed on in the cane fields:
carrion, blood, and a nausea
of harrowing petals.
Between coconut palms lay the graves, a stilled
strangulation, a festering surfeit of bones.
A finical satrap conversed
with wineglasses, collars, and piping.
In the palace, all flashed like a clock-dial,
precipitate laughter in gloves, a moment
spanning the passageways, meeting
the newly killed voices and the buried blue mouths. Out of
   sight,
lament was perpetual and fell, like a plant and its pollen,
forcing a lightless increase in the blinded, big leaves.
And bludgeon by bludgeon, on the terrible waters,
scale over scale in the bog,
the snout filled with silence and slime
and vendetta was born.

HAMBRE EN EL SUR

Veo el sollozo en el carbón de Lota
y la arrugada sombra del chileno humillado
picar la amarga veta de la entraña, morir,
vivir, nacer en la dura ceniza
agachados, caídos como si el mundo
entrara así y saliera así
entre polvo negro, entre llamas,
y sólo sucediera
la tos en el invierno, el paso
de un caballo en el agua negra, donde ha caído
una hoja de eucaliptus como un cuchillo muerto.

HUNGER IN THE SOUTH

Woe in the charcoals of Lota, I see:
the dishonored *chileno* like a black corrugation
rifling the bitter recesses,
dying or living, born to the pitiless cinder
in a posture of kneeling, felled
between fires and black powder,
as if worlds might create and undo themselves
for only a winter's survival of coughing,
or the step of a horse through the pitch-colored water, where
     lately
the perishing knives of the stripped eucalyptus have fallen.

QUIERO VOLVER AL SUR: 1941

Enfermo en Veracruz, recuerdo un día
del Sur, mi tierra, un día de plata
como un rápido pez en el agua del cielo.
Loncoche, Lonquimay, Carahue, desde arriba
esparcidos, rodeados por silencio y raíces,
sentados en sus tronos de cueros y maderas.
El Sur es un caballo echado a pique
coronado con lentos árboles y rocío,
cuando levanta el verde hocico caen las gotas,
la sombra de su cola moja el gran archipiélago
y en su intestino crece el carbón venerado.
Nunca más, dime, sombra, nunca más, dime, mano,
nunca más, dime, pie, puerta, pierna, combate,
trastornarás la selva, el camino, la espiga,
la niebla, el frío, lo que, azul, determinaba
cada uno de tus pasos sin cesar consumidos?
Cielo, déjame un día de estrella a estrella irme
pisando luz y pólvora, destrozando mi sangre
hasta llegar al nido de la lluvia!
                              Quiero ir
detrás de la madera por el río
Toltén fragante, quiero salir de los aserraderos,
entrar en las cantinas con los pies empapados,
guiarme por la luz del avellano eléctrico,
tenderme junto al excremento de las vacas,
morir y revivir mordiendo trigo.
                              Océano, tráeme
un día del Sur, un día agarrado a tus olas,
un día de árbol mojado, trae un viento
azul polar a mi bandera fría!

Ailing in Veracruz, I remember
southern weather, weather
of the fleet fish in the heavens of water,
silvered, in my own country.
Loncoche, Lonquimay, Carahue, large on the summits,
circled by roots and serenities,
chaired upon platforms of rawhide and timber.
South is a stallion, submerging,
in the gradual trees and the dew, garlanded:
green muzzle poised, dropping water,
rump in the great archipelagoes, shadowed
and shimmering, ceremonial coal in his bowels.
Shade: will you never—finger and limb: will you never—
rivalries, portals and footfalls: are you never
to startle the jungles, the pathways and corn tassels,
mist, and cerulean cold that appoints you
the range of your wayfaring, endlessly vanishing?
Sky: conjure the day when I move in an orbit of stars,
trampling the lights and the powders, consuming my blood
till I nest in the eyrie of rain.
                              Permit that I pass
from the Toltén's aroma of timber, from the tooth of the
        sawyer,
drenched to the footsoles, to enter the little cantinas.
Conduct me to light in the hazelnut's voltage,
measure my length in the offal of cattle
to die and be born again, biting the germens.
                              Bring out of Ocean
a day of the South, grapple a day from your waves,
day of the watery tree: and summon the polar blue wind
to melt in the cold of my colors!

Pablo Neruda / 165

Fundamentales aguas, paredes de agua, trébol
y avena combatida,
cordelajes ya unidos a la red de una noche
húmeda, goteante, salvajemente hilada,
gota desgarradora repetida en lamento,
cólera diagonal cortando cielo.
Galopan los caballos de perfume empapado,
bajo el agua, golpeando el agua, interviniéndola
con sus ramajes rojos de pelo, piedra y agua:
y el vapor acompaña como una leche loca
el agua endurecida con fugaces palomas.
No hay día sino los cisternales
del clima duro, del verde movimiento
y las patas anudan veloz tierra y transcurso
entre bestial aroma de caballo con lluvia.
Mantas, monturas, pellones agrupados
en sombrías granadas sobre los
ardientes lomos de azufre que golpean
la selva decidiéndola.
                    Más allá, más allá, más allá, más allá.
más allá, más allá, más allá, más alláaaaaa,
los jinetes derriban la lluvia, los jinetes
pasan bajo los avellanos amargos, la lluvia
tuerce en trémulos rayos su trigo sempiterno.
Hay luz del agua, relámpago confuso
derramado en la hoja, y del mismo sonido del galope
sale un agua sin vuelo, herida por la tierra.
Húmeda rienda, bóveda enramada,
pasos de pasos, vegetal nocturno
de estrellas rotas como hielo o luna, ciclónico caballo

HORSEMAN IN RAIN

Primordial waters: clover and oat striving, water-walls,
a meshing of cords in the net of the night,
in the barbarous weave of the damp, dropping water,
a rending of waterdrops, lamenting successions,
diagonal rage, cutting heaven.
Steeped in aromas, smashing the water, interposing
the roan of their gloss, like a foliage, between boulder and
    water,
the horses gallop in water,
their vapor attending, in a lunatic milk,
a stampede of doves that hardens, like water.
Not day, but a cistern
of obdurate weather, green agitations,
where hooves join a landscape of haste
with the lapse of the rain and the bestial aroma of horses.
Blankets and pommels, clustering cloak-furs,
seed-falls of darkness,
ablaze on the haunches of brimstone
that beat the considering jungle.
                        Beyond and beyond and beyond
and beyond and beyond and beyond and beyoooooond:
the horsemen demolish the rain, the horsemen
pass under the bittering hazelnut, the rain
weaves unperishing wheat in a shimmer of lusters.
Here is water's effulgence, confusion of lightning,
to spill on the leaf, here, from the noise of the gallop,
the water goes wounded to earth, without flight.
The bridle reins dampen: branch-covered archways,
footfalls of footfalls, an herbage of darkness
in splintering star-shapes, moonlike, icelike, a cyclone of
    horses

Pablo Neruda / 167

cubierto por las flechas como un helado espectro,
lleno de nuevas manos nacidas en la furia,
golpeante manzana rodeada por el miedo
y su gran monarquía de temible estandarte.

riddled with points like an icicle prism—
and born out of furor, the innocent fingers brim over,
the apple encompassing terror
and the terrible banners of empire, are smitten.

CRISTÓBAL MIRANDA
(*Palero-Tocopilla*)

Te conocí, Cristóbal, en las lanchas anchas
de la bahía, cuando baja
el salitre, hacia el mar, en la quemante
vestidura de un día de Noviembre.
Recuerdo aquella extática apostura,
los cerros de metal, el agua quieta.
Y sólo el hombre de las lanchas, húmedo
de sudor, moviendo nieve.
Nieve de los nitratos, derramada
sobre los hombros del dolor, cayendo
a la barriga ciega de las naves.
Allí, paleros, héroes de una aurora
carcomida por ácidos, sujeta
a los destinos de la muerte, firmes,
recibiendo el nitrato caudaloso.
Cristóbal, este recuerdo para ti.
Para los camaradas de la pala,
a cuyos pechos entra el ácido
y las emanaciones asesinas,
hinchando como águilas aplastadas
los corazones, hasta que cae el hombre,
hasta que rueda el hombre hacia las calles,
hacia las cruces rotas de la pampa.
Bien, no digamos más, Cristóbal, ahora
este papel que te recuerda, a todos,
a los lancheros de bahía, al hombre
ennegrecido de los barcos, mis ojos
van con vosotros en esta jornada
y mi alma es una pala que levanta
cargando y descargando sangre y nieve,
junto a vosotros, vidas del desierto.

CRISTÓBAL MIRANDA
(*Stevedore, Tocopilla*)

I knew you in the big bay boats, Cristóbal,
on a day when the niter
came down to the sea's edge, in November's
scalding investiture.
I remember some ravished serenity,
the summits of metal and the unmoving water;
and a man wetted down in his sweat,
moving a cargo of snow, whose trade is with boats.
For nitrate moved with the snow, shed
on the harrowing shoulders, blind in
the boatholds, and falling:
for the stevedores, the heroes of morning,
bitten with acids, death's
imminent timeservers, taking
the prodigal niter, unshaken.
Cristóbal: this keepsake's for you—
a shoveler's fellowship, hearts
tumid with strain; the unascending eagles
into whose breathing the acids
and homicide gases have entered:
for all good men brought down in the street,
who wheel
toward the broken cross of their *pampa*.
Cristóbal: no more of that now.
This paper commends you to all,
all mariners, men
blackened with boats in the bay. My eyes
go with yours in this stint,
my force in the heft of your shovel,
in a desert's subsistence—standing near to you,
loading the blood and the snow and unloading it.

Pablo Neruda / *171*

HACIA LOS MINERALES

Después a las altas piedras
de sal y de oro, a la enterrada
república de los metales
subí:
eran los dulces muros en que una
piedra se amarra con otra,
con un beso de barro oscuro.

Un beso entre piedra y piedra
por los caminos tutelares,
un beso de tierra y tierra
entre las grandes uvas rojas,
y como un diente junto a otro diente
la dentadura de la tierra
las pircas de materia pura,
las que llevan el interminable
beso de las piedras del río
a los mil labios del camino

Subamos desde la agricultura al oro.
Aquí tenéis los altos pedernales.

El peso de la mano es como un ave.
Un hombre, un ave, una substancia de aire,
de obstinación, de vuelo, de agonía,
un párpado tal vez, pero un combate.

Y de allí en la transversal cuna del oro,
en Punitaqui, frente a frente,
con los callados palanqueros
del pique, de la pala, ven,
Pedro, con tu paz de cuero,
ven, Ramírez, con tus abrasadas

TOWARD MINERAL

Then, to the brine and the gold,
the buried republics of metal,
on the uppermost stone
I ascended:
there the walls yielded, stone
cleaving to stone
in the shadowy kiss of the pitch.

A mating of boulders
on guardian thoroughfares,
earth meeting earth
in a bigness of reddening grapes,
fang over fang, closing
a continent's denture.
stockades of immaculate matter
bearing a river bed's rubble,
exhaustless embracement,
to the thousandfold mouth of the highway.

Let us climb to the gold from the tillage.
Here the flint sheer begins.

The hand's weight, the bird's weight, are one:
aerial substances, the bird or the man,
alike in their self-will, their flights, and their passions—
an eyelash's flicker, perhaps; but an agon.

Transverse in the gold incunabula,
from here into Punitaqui, Pedro,
face to face in a pile driver's silence
of pickax and shovel,
come with your rawhide tranquillity—
and you with inflammable fingers

manos que indagaron el útero
de las cerradas minerías,
salud, en las gradas, en
los calcáreos subterráneos
del oro, abajo en sus matrices,
quedaron vuestras digitales
herramientas marcadas con fuego.

who probe in the womb of the minepit's enclosure,
Ramirez: thrive there on the stairway
in calcareous underground gold
in whose matrix the mark of your calling persists,
your hand, like a tool scored with fire, from below.

EL POETA

Antes anduve por la vida, en medio
de un amor doloroso: antes retuve
una pequeña página de cuarzo
clavándome los ojos en la vida.
Compré bondad, estuve en el mercado
de la codicia, respiré las aguas
más sordas de la envidia, la inhumana
hostilidad de máscaras y seres.
Viví un mundo de ciénaga marina
en que la flor de pronto, la azucena
me devoraba en su temblor de espuma,
y donde puse el pie resbaló mi alma
hacia las dentaduras del abismo.
Así nació mi poesía, apenas
rescatada de ortigas, empuñada
sobre la soledad como un castigo,
o apartó en el jardín de la impudicia
su más secreta flor hasta enterrarla.
Aislado así como el agua sombría
que vive en sus profundos corredores,
corrí de mano en mano, al aislamiento
de cada ser, al odio cuotidiano,
Supe que así vivían, escondiendo
la mitad de los seres, como peces
del más extraño mar, y en las fangosas
inmensidades encontré la muerte.
La muerte abriendo puertas y caminos.
La muerte deslizándose en los muros.

THE POET

That time when I moved among happenings
in the midst of my mournful devotions; that time
when I cherished a leaflet of quartz,
at gaze in a lifetime's vocation.
I ranged in the markets of avarice
where goodness is bought for a price, breathed
the insensate miasmas of envy, the inhuman
contention of masks and existences.
I endured in the bog-dweller's element; the lily
that breaks on the water in a sudden
disturbance of bubbles and blossoms, devoured me.
Whatever the foot sought, the spirit deflected,
or sheered toward the fang of the pit.
So my poems took being, in travail
retrieved from the thorn, like a penance,
wrenched by a seizure of hands, out of solitude;
or they parted for burial
their secretest flower in immodesty's garden.
Estranged to myself, like shadow on water,
that moves through a corridor's fathoms,
I sped through the exile of each man's existence,
this way and that, and so, to habitual loathing;
for I saw that their being was this: to stifle
one half of existence's fullness like fish
in an alien limit of ocean. And there,
in immensity's mire, I encountered their death;
Death grazing the barriers,
Death opening roadways and doorways.

EL GRAN OCÉANO

Si de tus dones y de tus destrucciones, Océano, a mis manos
pudiera destinar una medida, una fruta, un fermento,
escogería tu reposo distante, las líneas de tu acero,
tu extensión vigilada por el aire y la noche,
y la energía de tu idioma blanco
que destroza y derriba sus columnas
en su propia pureza demolida.

    No es la última ola con su salado peso
    la que tritura costas y produce
    la paz de arena que rodea el mundo:
    es el central volumen de la fuerza,
    la potencia extendida de las aguas,
    la inmóvil soledad llena de vidas.
    Tiempo, tal vez, o copa acumulada
    de todo movimiento, unidad pura
    que no selló la muerte, verde víscera
    de la totalidad abrasadora.

Del brazo sumergido que levanta una gota
no queda sino un beso de la sal. De los cuerpos
del hombre en tus orillas una húmeda fragancia
de flor mojada permanece. Tu energía
parece resbalar sin ser gastada,
parece regresar a su reposo.

La ola que desprendes,
arco de identidad, pluma estrellada,
cuando se despeñó fué sólo espuma,
y regresó a nacer sin consumirse.

OPEN SEA

If, to my hands, from its havocs and bounties,
the Sea might appoint me a ferment, a portion, a fruit,
I would speak for that concord of distance, perspectives of
   steel,
evenings and airs of alerted extension—
your power, like a language of whiteness, O Ocean,
the spoilure and rending of columns,
into innocent essence brought low.

   Not yet that ultimate wave in the weight of its brine,
   smashing on seacoast, conducing
   the peace of the sand that encircles a world.
   But power and volume concenter,
   capacity ranges the waters,
   unmoved, in the flowing aloneness, in a surfeit of lives:
   Time, it may be, or the goblet of motion's entirety,
   upgathered and brimless with death; original singlehood,
   visceral greens,
   in a charring totality.

The drowned arm, uplifting,
carries only the kiss of the salt in a droplet. From the torsos
   of men,
a humid perfume on the beaches,
the soaked flower, retained;
your power in a semblance of squandering force,
undiminished, returned in a semblance of calm.

Your wave, giving way
in a bow of identity, explosion of feathers,
a trifle of spindrift, expends itself headlong
and returns to its cause, unconsumed.

Pablo Neruda / 179

Toda tu fuerza vuelve a ser origen.
Sólo entregas despojos triturados,
cáscaras que apartó tu cargamento,
lo que expulsó la acción de tu abundancia,
todo lo que dejó de ser racimo.

Tu estatua está extendida más allá de las olas.

Viviente y ordenada como el pecho y el manto
de un solo ser y sus respiraciones,
en la materia de la luz izadas,
llanuras levantadas por las olas,
forman la piel desnuda del planeta.

Llenas tu propio ser con tu substancia.
Colmas la curvatura del silencio.

Con tu sal y tu miel tiembla la copa,
la cavidad universal del agua,
y nada falta en ti como en el cráter
desollado, en el vaso cerril:
cumbres vacías, cicatrices, señales
que vigilan el aire mutilado.

Tus pétalos palpitan contra el mundo,
tiemblan tus cereales submarinos,
las suaves ovas cuelgan su amenaza,
navegan y pululan las escuelas,
y sólo sube al hilo de las redes
el relámpago muerto de la escama,
un milímetro herido en la distancia
de tus totalidades cristalinas.

And vigor recovers its origin.
No more than a ruined excess you surrender, O **Sea**:
your burden breaks only a husk,
whatever mobility freed from abundance
or lifted itself from the cluster.

Farther than sea-surge your form is extended.

Ardent and ordered, like a gesture of breathing
on breast and its vesture, out of isolate being,
borne up into tissue of light,
your meadows arise on the billow
and the flesh of a planet is bared.

Substance of selfhood overflows into being.
The crescent of silence is brimmed.

The goblet is shaken with salt and with honey,
creation's abysm of waters,
and nothing is lacking, O Sea! Here is no crater's
dismemberment in the cup of the headlands,
no pinnacle's emptiness, vestiges, scars,
patroling an air's mutilation.

The petals of ocean contend with a planet's pulsation.
The underseas granaries tremble.
A gloss on the sea-lettuce poises its menace,
a swimming and swarming of schools;
the mesh of the net-cord, ascending,
draws up only a fish scale's extinction of lightning
one wounded gradation of distance,
in the crystal's accomplished perfection.

LEVIATHAN

Arca, paz iracunda, resbalada
noche bestial, antártica extranjera,
no pasarás junto a mí desplazando
tu témpano de sombra sin que un día
entre por tus paredes y levante
tu armadura de invierno submarino.

Hacia el Sur crepitó tu fuego negro
de expulsado planeta, el territorio
de tu silencio que movió las algas
sacudiendo la edad de la espesura.

Fué sólo forma, magnitud cerrada
por un temblor del mundo en que desliza
su majestad de cuero amedrentado
por su propia potencia y su ternura.

Arca de cólera encendida
con las antorchas de la nieve negra,
cuando tu sangre ciega fué fundada
la edad del mar dormía en los jardines,
y en su extensión la luna deshacía
la cola de su imán fosforescente.
La vida crepitaba
como una hoguera azul, madre medusa,
multiplicada tempestad de ovarios,
y todo el crecimiento era pureza,
palpitación de pámpano marino.

Así fué tu gigante arboladura
dispuesta entre las aguas como el paso
de la maternidad sobre la sangre,
y tu poder fué noche inmaculada

LEVIATHAN

Ark on the waters, fury at peace with itself, derelict
night of the brute, antarctic outlander,
nearing and passing me—an ice field
displacing in darkness—one day
I shall enter your walls, I shall salvage
the sunken marine of your winter, your armory.

Southward, there crackled a holocaust, black
with your planet's expulsion, the domains
of your silence that moved in the algae
and jostled the densities.

Then, form was, alone: magnitudes
sealed by a world's agitation, wherein glided
your leathern pre-eminence, mistrusting
the gifts of its nature: tenderness, power.

Ark of our passion, striking fire
in the blackening snow, as with torches,
when your blind blood was quickened
an epoch of ocean still slept in its gardens,
and in an immensity the disfiguring moon
divided its track like a magnet of phosphor.
Life sputtered,
the mother-medusa, blue in the flame,
a tempest of multiple wombs,
and increase grew whole in its purity,
a pompano's pulse in the sea.

Among waters, your congress
of mastheads and spars was disposed
like maternity's motion in blood,
and your power of inviolate night

Pablo Neruda / 183

que resbaló inundando las raíces.
Extravío y terror estremecieron
la soledad, y huyó tu continente
más allá de las islas esperadas:
pero el terror pasó sobre los globos
de la luna glacial, y entró en tu carne,
agredió soledades que ampararon
tu aterradora lámpara apagada.
La noche fué contigo: te envolvía
adhiriéndote un limo tempestuoso
y revolvió tu cola huracanada
el hielo en que dormían las estrellas.

Oh gran herida, manantial caliente
revolviendo sus truenos derrotados
en la comarca del arpón, teñido
por el mar de la sangre, desangrada,
dulce y dormida bestia conducida
como un ciclón de rotos hemisferios
hasta las barcas negras de la grasa
pobladas por rencor y pestilencia.

Oh gran estatua muerta en los cristales
de la luna polar, llenando el cielo
como una nube de terror que llora
y cubre los océanos de sangre.

was shed on the roots in a deluge.
Past expectancy's islands, your continent
fled, dereliction and terror
made the loneliness tremble:
even so, terror mounted the globes
of the glacial moon, terror entered your flesh
and struck at your solitude, the asylums
of dread where your lamp lay extinguished.
With you was the night: a tempestuous slime
that held you like pitch and enveloped you
while your tail's hurricano
spun the ice of a slumbering galaxy.

O enormously wounded one! fiery fountainhead
lashing a ruin of thunders,
on the harpoon's periphery, stained
in the blood bath, bleeding all virtue away,
the repose and the calm of the animal conduct you,
a cyclone of fracturing crescents,
to the black boats of blubber
and the creatures of rancor and plague.

Great mold among crystals dead
on a pole of the moon, heaven itself is encompassed,
pandemonium's cloud that laments there
and covers all ocean with blood.

LOS ENIGMAS

Me habéis preguntado qué hila el crustáceo
   entre sus patas de oro
y os respondo: El mar lo sabe.
Me decís qué espera la ascidia en su campana transparente?
   Qué espera?
Yo os digo, espera como vosotros el tiempo.
Me preguntáis a quién alcanza el abrazo del alga
   Macrocustis?
Indagadlo, indagadlo a cierta hora, en cierto mar que
   conozco.
Sin duda me preguntaréis por el marfil maldito del narwhal,
   para que yo os conteste
de qué modo el unicornio marino agoniza arponeado.
Me preguntáis tal vez por las plumas alcionarias que
   tiemblan
en los puros orígenes de la marea austral?
Y sobre la construcción cristalina del pólipo habéis barajado,
   sin duda
una pregunta más, desgranándola ahora?
Queréis saber la eléctrica materia de las púas del fondo?
La armada estalactita que camina quebrándose?
El anzuelo del pez pescador, la música extendida
en la profundidad como un hilo en el agua?

Yo os quiero decir que esto lo sabe el mar, que la vida en sus
   arcas
es ancha como la arena, innumerable y pura
y entre las uvas sanguinarias el tiempo ha pulido
la dureza de un pétalo, la luz de la medusa
y ha desgranado el ramo de sus hebras corales
desde una cornucopia de nácar infinito.

THE ENIGMAS

You would know what the crab in its claw-holds of gold
    weaves,
and I answer: Ocean will say it.
You ask what the luminous bell of the tunicate awaits in the
    water: what
does it hope for? I tell you, it waits for the fullness of time,
    like yourself.
For whom does the alga Macrocystis extend its embraces?
Unriddle it, riddle it out, at a time, in a sea that I know.
And the narwhal's malevolent ivory? though you turn for
    my answer, I tell you
you stay for a stranger reply; how he suffered the killing
    harpoon.
Or you look, it may be, for the kingfisher's plumage, a pul-
    sation
of purest beginning in the tropical water.
Now, on the lucid device of the polyp you tangle
a new importunity, flailing it fine, to the bran:
you would sift the electrical matter that moves on the tines
    of the void;
the stalactite's splintering armor that lengthens its crystal;
the barb of the angler fish, the singing extension
that weaves in the depths and is loosed on the waters?

I would answer you: Ocean will say it—the arc of its life-
    time
is vast as the sea-sand, flawless and numberless.
Between cluster and cluster, the blood and the vintage,
    time brightens
the flint in the petal, the beam in the jellyfish;
the branches are threshed in the skein of the coral
from the infinite pearl of the horn.

Pablo Neruda / 187

Yo no soy sino la red vacía que adelanta
ojos humanos, muertos en aquellas tinieblas,
dedos acostumbrados al triángulo, medidas
de un tímido hemisferio de naranja.

Anduve como vosotros escarbando
la estrella interminable,
y en mi red, en la noche, me desperté desnudo,
única presa, pez encerrado en el viento.

I am that net waiting emptily—out of range
of the onlooker, slain in the shadows,
fingers inured to a triangle, a timid
half-circle's dimensions computed in oranges.

Probing a starry infinitude,
I came, like yourselves,
through the mesh of my being, in the night, and awoke to
    my nakedness—
all that was left of the catch—a fish in the noose of the wind.

Odas Elementales / Elemental Odes
Series I, II, III
(1954-1957)

ODA A LA ALCACHOFA

La alcachofa
de tierno corazón
se vistió de guerrero,
erecta, construyó
una pequeña cúpula,
se mantuvo
impermeable
bajo
sus escamas,
a su lado
los vegetales locos
se encresparon,
se hicieron
zarcillos, espadañas,
bulbos conmovedores,
en el subsuelo
durmió la zanahoria
de bigotes rojos,
la viña
resecó los sarmientos
por donde sube el vino,
la col
se dedicó
a probarse faldas,
el orégano
a perfumar el mundo,
y la dulce
alcachofa
allí en el huerto,
vestida de guerrero,
bruñida
como una granada,
orgullosa;

ARTICHOKE

The artichoke
of delicate heart
erect
in its battle-dress, builds
its minimal cupola;
keeps
stark
in its scallop of
scales.
Around it,
demoniac vegetables
bristle their thicknesses,
devise
tendrils and belfries,
the bulb's agitations;
while under the subsoil
the carrot
sleeps sound in its
rusty mustaches.
Runner and filaments
bleach in the vineyards,
whereon rise the vines.
The sedulous cabbage
arranges
its petticoats;
oregano
sweetens a world;
and the artichoke
dulcetly there in a gardenplot,
armed for a skirmish,
goes proud
in its pomegranate
burnishes.

Pablo Neruda / 193

y un día
una con otra
en grandes cestos
de mimbre, caminó
por el mercado
a realizar su sueño:
la milicia.
En hileras
nunca fué tan marcial
como en la feria,
los hombres
entre las legumbres
con sus camisas blancas
eran
mariscales
de las alcachofas,
las filas apretadas,
las voces de comando,
y la detonación
de una caja que cae;

pero
entonces
viene
María
con su cesto,
escoge
una alcachofa,
no le teme,
la examina, la observa
contra la luz como si fuera un huevo,
la compra,
la confunde
en su bolsa

Till, on a day,
each by the other,
the artichoke moves
to its dream
of a market place
in the big willow
hoppers:
a battle formation.
Most warlike
of defilades—
with men
in the market stalls,
white shirts
in the soup-greens,
artichoke
field marshals,
close-order conclaves,
commands, detonations,
and voices,
a crashing of crate staves.

And
Maria
come
down
with her hamper
to
make trial
of an artichoke:
she reflects, she examines,
she candles them up to the light like an egg,
never flinching;
she bargains,
she tumbles her prize
in a market bag

con un par de zapatos,
con un repollo y una
botella
de vinagre
hasta
que entrando a la cocina
la sumerge en la olla.

Así termina
en paz
esta carrera
del vegetal armado
que se llama alcachofa,
luego
escama por escama,
desvestimos
la delicia
y comemos
la pacífica pasta
de su corazón verde.

among shoes and a
cabbage head,
a bottle
of vinegar; is back
in her kitchen.
The artichoke drowns in an olla.

So you have it:
a vegetable, armed,
a profession
(call it an artichoke)
whose end
is millennial.
We taste of that
sweetness,
dismembering
scale after scale.
We eat of a halcyon paste:
it is green at the artichoke heart.

ODA A UN RELOJ EN LA NOCHE

En la noche, en tu mano
brilló como luciérnaga
mi reloj.
Oí
su cuerda:
como un susurro seco
salía
de tu mano invisible.
Tu mano entonces
volvió a mi pecho oscuro
a recoger mi sueño y su latido.

El reloj
siguió cortando el tiempo
con su pequeña sierra.
Como en un bosque
caen
fragmentos de madera,
mínimas gotas, trozos
de ramajes o nidos,
sin que cambie el silencio,
sin que la fresca oscuridad termine;

así
siguió el reloj cortando
desde tu mano invisible,
tiempo, tiempo,
y cayeron
minutos como hojas,
fibras de tiempo roto,
pequeñas plumas negras.

A WATCH IN THE NIGHT

Nighttime: my watch dial
burns on your hand
like a glowworm.
I hear
the stretched filament:
like a dry exhalation
that escapes
your invisible hand.
Then your hand
turning back to my breast in the dark
to gather my dream to its breathing.

A delicate tooth
in the watch
saws at a lifetime.
Somewhere in the forest
the fragments are falling:
splinters of wood,
infinitesimal droppings, parings
and nests in the leafage—
but the stillness is changeless,
the chill in the dark does not lessen.

So
from invisible hands
a wristwatch goes whittling
a lifetime,
a lifetime,
the minutes falling like leaves,
fibers of ruining time,
little black plumules.

Pablo Neruda / 199

Como en el bosque
olíamos raíces,
el agua en algún sitio desprendía
una gotera gruesa
como uva mojada.
Un pequeño molino
molía noche,
la sombra susurraba
cayendo de tu mano
y llenaba la tierra.
Polvo,
tierra, distancia
molía y molía
mi reloj en la noche,
desde tu mano.

Yo puse
mi brazo
bajo tu cuello invisible,
bajo su peso tibio
y en mi mano
cayó el tiempo,
la noche,
pequeños ruidos
de madera y de bosque,
de noche dividida,
de fragmentos de sombra,
de agua que cae y cae:

entonces
cayó el sueño
desde el reloj y desde
tus dos manos dormidas,
cayó como agua oscura
de los bosques,

As though in a forest
we turned with the odor of roots in our nostrils
and somewhere heard water give way
in thickening droplets
like the ooze on a grape.
The smallest of millstones
is milling the night.
The darkness is murmurous,
sifting down from your hand
and brimming the universe—
distances,
dust, and the earth:
the grindstone goes grinding,
my watch on your hand
in the dark.

Blindly
I steady my arm
for your neck, move
under the warmth and weight of your body,
and into my hands
time topples downward—
a night
of diminutive noises,
wood-noises, tree-noises,
night-noises, dividing,
fragments of darkness,
a falling and falling away of the waters.

Till
out of your watch
and the sleep of your hands
the dream of the sleeper falls downward,
falls darkling, a gush
in the forest;

Pablo Neruda / 201

del reloj
a tu cuerpo,
de ti hacia los países,
agua oscura,
tiempo que cae
y corre
adentro de nosotros.

Y así fué aquella noche,
sombra y espacio, tierra
y tiempo,
algo que corre y cae
y pasa.
Y así todas las noches
van por la tierra,
no dejan sino un vago
aroma negro,
cae una hoja,
una gota
en la tierra
apaga su sonido,
duerme el bosque, las aguas,
las praderas,
las campanas,
los ojos.

Te oigo y respiras,
amor mío:

dormimos.

out of your watch
to your body,
out of your flesh to the
countries of darkening water:
time falling,
time coursing us there
from within.

The whole night was like that.
Spaces and shadows, the turning
of time and the earth:
something flooding and flowing
and falling away.
So pass the nights
of the earth,
leaving no more than a vagrant
black odor:
a leaf falls,
a drop falls
to earth
and the sound of it perishes;
sleep falls on the woods and the waters,
on the meadows,
the bells,
and the eyelids.

Breathe, and I hear you,
my darling.

Let us sleep.

ODA AL NIÑO DE LA LIEBRE

A la luz del otoño
en el camino
el niño
levantaba en sus manos
no una flor
ni una lámpara
sino una liebre muerta.

Los motores rayaban
la carretera fría,
los rostros no miraban
detrás
de los cristales,
eran ojos
de hierro,
orejas
enemigas,
rápidos dientes
que relampagueaban
resbalando
hacia el mar y las ciudades,
y el niño
del otoño
con su liebre,
huraño
como un cardo,
duro
como una piedrecita,
allí
levantando
una mano
hacia la exhalación
de los viajeros.

BOY WITH A HARE

In fall light
and the highway,
a child
holding up in his hands
not lanterns
or petals
but the death of a hare.

Motorcars rake
the cold causeways.
Faces are glazed
under
windshields,
eyeballs
of metal
and inimical
ears,
teeth hurrying,
crackling their lightning,
sheering away to the sea and the cities;
and a child
with a hare
in the autumn,
shy
as a
thistle seed,
rigid
as flint,
lifting
his hand
to the
fume
of the motorcade.

Pablo Neruda / *205*

Nadie
se detenía.

Eran pardas
las altas cordilleras,
cerros
color de puma
perseguido,
morado
era
el silencio
y como
dos ascuas
de diamante
negro
eran
los ojos
del niño con su liebre,
dos puntas
erizadas
de cuchillo,
dos cuchillitos negros,
eran los ojos
del niño,
allí perdido
ofreciendo su liebre
en el inmenso
otoño
del camino.

Nobody
slackens.

It is tawny
up on the ridges,
on the summit,
the hues
of a puma, pursued.
The silence
goes
violet.
Like
cinders, black diamonds,
the eyes
of the child and the hare,
two
knife-points
upright
on a knifeblade,
two little black poniards,
the eyes
of a little child
lost,
who
proffers
the death of a hare
in the towering
fall
of the road.

ODA AL OLOR DE LA LEÑA

Tarde, con las estrellas
abiertas en el frío
abrí la puerta.
                    El mar
galopaba
en la noche.

Como una mano
de la casa oscura
salió el aroma
intenso
de la leña guardada.

Visible era el aroma
como
si el árbol
estuviera vivo.
Como si todavía palpitara.

Visible
como una vestidura.

Visible
como una rama rota.

Anduve
adentro
de la casa
rodeado
por aquella balsámica
oscuridad.
Afuera
las puntas

A SMELL OF CORDWOOD

Later, when stars
opened out to the cold,
I opened the door.
                    Night:
on an ocean
of galloping hooves.

Then from the dark
of the house, like a hand,
the savage
aroma
of wood on the woodpile.

An odor
that lives
like a tree,
a visible odor.
As if cordwood pulsed like a tree.

Vesture
made visible.

A visible
breaking of branches.

I turned back
to
the house
in the circle
of darkening
balsam.
Beyond,
a sparkle

del cielo cintilaban
como piedras magnéticas,
y el olor de la leña
me tocaba
el corazón
como unos dedos,
como un jazmín,
como algunos recuerdos.

No era el olor agudo
de los pinos,
no,
no era
la ruptura en la piel
del eucaliptus,
no eran
tampoco
los perfumes verdes
de la viña,
sino
algo más secreto,
porque aquella fragancia
una sola,
una sola
vez existía,
y allí, de todo lo que vi en el mundo,
en mi propia
casa, de noche, junto al mar de invierno,
allí estaba esperándome
el olor
de la rosa más profunda,
el corazón cortado de la tierra,
algo
que me invadió como una ola
desprendida

of motes in the sky,
like lodestones.
But the wood-smell
took hold of
my heart,
like a hand and its fingers,
like jasmine,
like a memory cherished.

Not harrowing
pine-odor,
not that way,
not slashed
eucalyptus,
not like
the green
exhalation
of arbors—
but
something more recondite,
a fragrance
that gives itself
once, and once
only,
among all things visible,
a world
or a house, a night
by the wintering water:
that awaited me there,
occult in the smell
of the rose,
an earth-heart plucked out,
dominion
that struck like a wave,
a sundered

del tiempo
y se perdió en mí mismo
cuando yo abrí la puerta
de la noche.

duration,
and was lost in my blood
when I opened the door
of the night.

ODA AL ACEITE

Cerca del rumoroso
cereal, de las olas
del viento en las avenas,

el olivo

de volumen plateado,
severo en su linaje,
en su torcido
corazón terrestre:
las gráciles
olivas
pulidas
por los dedos
que hicieron
la paloma
y el caracol
marino:
verdes,
innumerables,
purísimos
pezones
de la naturaleza,
y allí
en
los secos
olivares,
donde
tan sólo
cielo azul con cigarras,
y tierra dura
existen,
allí

IN PRAISE OF OIL

Near the cereal
hum, undulations
of wind in the oat fields

a bulking of silver

the olive
of rigorous kindred,
a terrestrial knot
at its heart:
the felicitous
olive
stainless
as though from the fingers
that summoned
the snail
from the sea,
and the dove:
creation's
immaculate
nipple
in numberless
greens,
in
the drouth
of the olive grove
where
only
the azure, cicada and sky,
endure
on the obdurate
cobble—

el prodigio,
la cápsula
perfecta
de la oliva
llenando
con sus constelaciones el follaje:
más tarde
las vasijas,
el milagro,
el aceite.

Yo amo
las patrias del aceite,
los olivares
de Chacabuco, en Chile,
en la mañana
las plumas de platino
forestales
contra las arrugadas
cordilleras,
en Anacapri, arriba,
sobre la luz tirrena,
la desesperación de los olivos,
y en el mapa de Europa,
España,
cesta negra de aceitunas
espolvoreada por los azahares
como por una ráfaga marina.

Aceite
recóndita y suprema
condición de la olla,
pedestal de perdices,
llave celeste de la mayonesa,

that prodigy
there,
the sheath
of the consummate
olive,
zodiacs
filling the leaves:
and later,
a vessel
of miracle,
the dropping of oil.

I have loved
the dominions of oil:
Chacabuco's Chilean
groves,
platinum plumes
in the morning,
a forest of feathers,
on the peak's
crenelations;
on in Anacapri,
in Tyrrhenian dazzle, aloft,
the despairs of the olive;
or the Spain
of the map-maker's Europe,
a blackening basket of olives
seen among lemon leaves,
like a powdery gust from the sea.

Oil for
an olla's
epiphany,
the partridge's pedestal,
keys to a mayonnaise heaven,

suave y sabroso
sobre las lechugas
y sobrenatural en el infierno
de los arzobispales pejerreyes.
Aceite, en nuestra voz, en
nuestro coro,
con
íntima
suavidad poderosa
cantas:
eres idioma
castellano:
hay sílabas de aceite,
hay palabras
útiles y olorosas
como tu fragante materia.

No sólo canta el vino,
también canta el aceite,
vive en nosotros con su luz madura
y entre los bienes de la tierra
aparto,
aceite,
tu inagotable paz, tu esencia verde,
tu colmado tesoro que desciende
desde los manantiales del olivo.

the bland and the savory
over the lettuce leaf—
supernatural, too, in the hells
of the archiepiscopal mackerel.
Oil in our voices,
our singing assemblage
intoning
the might
of your intimate
suavity;
and Castilian,
that language of oil:
oleaginous syllables,
the needful, ambrosial
words
like your redolent substances.

For the olive
will sing with the wine:
the ripening light will inhabit us.
Out of earth's providence
I unbind
inexhaustible peace from the oil,
irreducible green,
the treasured excess moving down to us,
the gout welling up in the oil.

Con esos
pies
pequeños
parecidos
a abejas,
cómo
gastas
zapatos!

Ya sé
que vas y vienes,
que corres las escalas,
que adelantas al viento.
Antes
de que
te llame
ya has llegado,
y junto a la agresiva
cintura de la costa,
arena, piedra, espinas,
vas
a mi lado,
en los bosques
pisando troncos, mudas
aguas verdes,
o en las calles
andando
intransitables
suburbios, pavimentos
de alquitrán fatigado,
a esa hora
en que la luz
del mundo
se deshilacha como

YOU FLAME-FOOT!

Those feet of yours—
pint-sized,
no bigger
than bees,
how
they
eat up
the shoe leather!

Granted:
your comings and goings;
you hurtle up ladders
and outdistance the wind:
you
are
there
before one can call to you.
Close to the punishing
belt of the coastlands—
the rubble, the thorn and the sand—
you go
dogging my heels
in the timberlands,
striding on tree trunks through
the muted green water;
or you cross
the uncrossable
streets
of suburbia, the defeated
macadam of pavements
at an hour
when the light
on a planet
unravels itself like

Pablo Neruda / 221

una bandera,
tú, por calles y bosques,
a mi lado
caminas,
bravía, inagotable
compañera,
pero,
Dios mío!
cómo gastas
zapatos!

Apenas
me parece
que llegaron
en su caja
y al abrirla
salieron
bruñidos
como dos
pequeñas herramientas
de combate,
intactos
como
dos monedas
de
oro,
como dos campanitas,
y hoy,
qué veo?

En tus pies
dos erizos
arrugados,
dos puños entreabiertos,
dos informes
pepinos,

a pennon,
everywhere close to me,
treading
pavement and forests,
tameless and tireless
wayfarer—
but
Lord!
how you eat
up the shoe leather!

For example:
the shoe box has hardly
arrived
with the shoes.
I open the shoe box!
Presto! Two
little weapons
with a rifleman's
polish,
all of a piece,
like a
coin—
gold
of the
realm;
like two little bells—
then
what do I see?

Two feet
like a tangle of porcupines,
two half-opened fists,
two slovenly
cucumbers,

dos batracios
de cuero
desteñido,
eso,
eso
han llegado
a ser
los dos luceros
hace un mes, solo un mes
salidos
de la zapatería.

Como
flor amarilla de hermosura,
abierta en la barranca,
o enredadera viva en el ramaje,
como
la calceolaria
o el copihue
o como el amaranto electrizado,
así,
mi cristalina, mi fragante,
así tú, floreciendo, me acompañas,
y una pajarería, una cascada
de los australes
montes
es
tu corazón
cantando
junto al mío,
pero,
como
te comes
los zapatos,
Pies de Fuego!

two discolored
and leathery amphibians:
that's
what
we've
come
to—
that's what becomes
of two stars in a galaxy
a month ago—hardly a month ago—
fresh
from the cobbler.

Imagine
a blossom:
it breaks in a hollow
and yellows some loveliness there;
a climber alive in the branches:
calceolaria,
copihue,
electrified amaranth—
you came to me that way,
transparently, fragrantly,
a blossomer; we traveled together.
A cascade
from a glacial
summit, an aviary,
your heart
singing
next to my own.
But—
say, little Flame-Foot!
how
you eat
up
the shoe leather!

ODA AL BUZO

Salió el hombre de goma
de los mares.

Sentado
parecía
rey
redondo
del agua,
pulpo
secreto
y gordo,
talle
tronchado
de invisible alga.

Del oceánico bote
bajaron
pescadores
harapientos,
morados
por la noche
en el océano,
bajaron
levantando
largos peces fosfóricos
como
fuego voltaico,
los erizos cayendo
amontonaron
sobre las arenas
el rencor quebradizo
de sus púas.

DIVER

The rubber man
rose from the sea.

Seated,
he seemed
like a globular
king
of the waters,
a bulbous
and secretive
cuttlefish,
the truncated
device
of invisible algae.

From their boats, in mid-ocean,
the fishermen
sink
in their rags,
blue
with the night
of the ocean:
around them arise
the great fish of phosphor,
a voltage
of fire,
they go under:
around them, the sea urchins
tumble, piling
the silt
with the splintering spite
of their hackles.

Pablo Neruda / 227

El hombre
submarino
sacó sus grandes piernas,
torpemente
tambaleó entre intestinos
horribles de pescado.
Las gaviotas cortaban
el aire libre con
sus veloces tijeras,
y el buzo
como un ebrio
caminaba
en la playa,
torpe
y hosco,
enfundado
no sólo
en su vestido de cetáceo,
sino aún
medio mar
y medio tierra,
sin saber cómo
dirigir los inmensos
pies de goma.

Allí estaba naciendo.
Se desprendió
del mar
como del útero,
inocente,
y era sombrío, débil
y salvaje,
como
un
recién
nacido.

The underseas
man
thrashes the breadth of his legs;
languidly
reels
in the horror of fish gut:
gulls
slash
the limitless air
with their hurrying scissors;
the diver
toils
through the sand
like a drunkard,
swarthy
and comatose,
locked
into his clothing, cetacean,
half-earthen,
half-ocean,
going nowhere,
inept
in the rubbery bulk
of his feet.

He goes on to his birth-throes.
The ocean
gives way
like a womb
to this innocent:
he floats sullen
and strengthless
and barbarous,
like
the
newly born.

Pablo Neruda / *229*

Cada vez
le tocaba
nacer
para las aguas
o la arena.
Cada día
bajando
de la proa
a las crueles
corrientes,
al frío
del Pacífico
chileno,
el buzo
tenía
que nacer,
hacerse
monstruo,
sombra
avanzar
con cautela,
aprender
a moverse
con lentitud
de luna
submarina,
tener
apenas
pensamientos
de agua,
recoger
los hostiles
frutos, estalactitas,
o tesoros
de la profunda soledad

Time after time
he takes hold of the water, the sand,
and is
born again.
Submerging
each day
to the hold
of the pitiless
current,
Pacific and
Chilean
cold,
the diver
must practice
his
birth again,
make himself
monstrous
and tentative,
displace himself
fearfully,
grow wise
in his slothful
mobility, like
an underseas
moon.
Even
his thinking
must merge
with the water:
he harvests
inimical
fruits, stalactites,
treasures,
in the pit of a solitude

de aquellos
mojados
cementerios,
como si recogiera
coliflores,
y cuando como un globo
de aire negro
subía
hacia
la luz, hacia
su Mercedes,
su Clara, su Rosaura,
era difícil
andar,
pensar, comer
de nuevo.
Todo
era comienzo
para
aquel hombre tan grande
todavía inconcluso,
tambaleante
entre la oscuridad
de dos abismos.

Como todas las cosas
que aprendí
en mi existencia,
viéndolas, conociendo,
aprendí que ser buzo
es un oficio
difícil? No!
Infinito.

drenched
with the wash
of those graveyards—
as others
would turn up a cauliflower,
he comes up
to the light—
black air in a bubble—
to Mercedes,
Clara, Rosaura.
It is painful
to walk like a man again,
to think as a man thinks, to eat
again.
All
is beginning again
for
the bulking,
ambiguous man
staggering still
in the dark
of two different abysses.

This I know—
do I not?—
as I know my existence: all
things I have seen and considered.
The way of the diver
is hazardous? The vocation
is
infinite.

ODA AL LIMÓN

De aquellos azahares
desatados
por la luz de la luna,
de aquel
olor de amor
exasperado,
hundido en la fragancia,
salió
del limonero el amarillo,
desde su planetario
bajaron a la tierra los limones.

Tierna mercadería!
Se llenaron las costas,
los mercados,
de luz, de oro
silvestre,
y abrimos
dos mitades
de milagro,
ácido congelado
que corría
desde los hemisferios
de una estrella,
y el licor más profundo
de la naturaleza,
intransferible, vivo,
irreductible
nació de la frescura
del limón,
de su casa fragante,
de su ácida, secreta simetría.

A LEMON

Out of lemon flowers
loosed
on the moonlight, love's
lashed and insatiable
essences,
sodden with fragrance,
the lemon tree's yellow
emerges,
the lemons
move down
from the tree's planetarium.

Delicate merchandise!
The harbors are big with it—
bazaars
for the light and the
barbarous gold.
We open
the halves
of a miracle,
and a clotting of acids
brims
into the starry
divisions:
creation's
original juices,
irreducible, changeless,
alive:
so the freshness lives on
in a lemon,
in the sweet-smelling house of the rind,
the proportions, arcane and acerb.

En el limón cortaron
los cuchillos
una pequeña
catedral,
el ábside escondido
abrió a la luz los ácidos vitrales
y en gotas
resbalaron los topacios,
los altares,
la fresca arquitectura.

Así, cuando tu mano
empuña el hemisferio
del cortado
limón sobre tu plato
un universo de oro
derramaste,
una
copa amarilla
con milagros,
uno de los pezones olorosos
del pecho de la tierra,
el rayo de la luz que se hizo fruta,
el fuego diminuto de un planeta.

Cutting the lemon
the knife
leaves a little
cathedral:
alcoves unguessed by the eye
that open acidulous glass
to the light; topazes
riding the droplets,
altars,
aromatic façades.

So, while the hand
holds the cut of the lemon,
half a world
on a trencher,
the gold of the universe
wells
to your touch:
a cup yellow
with miracles,
a breast and a nipple
perfuming the earth;
a flashing made fruitage,
the diminutive fire of a planet.

ODA AL DOBLE OTOÑO

Está viviendo el mar mientras la tierra
no tiene movimiento:
el grave otoño
de la costa
cubre
con su muerte
la luz inmóvil
de la tierra,
pero
el mar errante, el mar
sigue viviendo.

No hay
una
sola
gota
de
sueño,
muerte
o
noche
en su
combate:
todas
las máquinas
del agua, las azules
calderas,
las crepitantes fábricas
del viento
coronando
las olas
con

DOUBLE AUTUMN

Though the sea lives, the land
keeps immobile:
the coastland's
disconsolate autumns
that conceal
in their dying
the immutable light
of the earth;
but
the sea, the sea in its vagrancy,
goes on with its living.

Not
a droplet
is
lost
upon
dreaming,
not
death
or
the night,
in that
warfare:
all
the machines
of the water, the caldrons
of azure,
the crackling contexture
of sea-wind
that garlands
the wave
with

sus violentas flores,
todo
vivo
como
las vísceras
del toro,
como
el fuego
en la música,
como
el acto
de la unión amorosa.

Siempre fueron oscuros
los
trabajos
del otoño
en la tierra;
inmóviles
raíces, semillas
sumergidas
en el tiempo
y arriba
sólo
la corola del frío,
un vago
aroma de hojas
disolviéndose
en
oro:
nada.
Una hacha
en el bosque
rompe
un tronco de cristales,

its violent gardens—
all
lives
as
the viscera lives
in the bull,
like fire
lives in music,
like
the coupling
and thrust of desire.

The labors
of autumn
were always
occult
in the ground,
immovable
roots, the seedling
submerged
in its time,
with only
the freezing corolla
above,
a nondescript
odor of leaves
dissolving itself
in
the gold:
nothing at all.
Somewhere in the wood,
an ax
splits
a trunk into crystals:

luego
cae
la tarde
y la tierra
pone sobre su rostro
una máscara
negra.

Pero
el mar
no descansa, no duerme, no se ha muerto.
Crece en la noche
su barriga
que combaron
las estrellas
mojadas, como trigo en el alba,
crece,
palpita
y llora
como un niño
perdido
que sólo con el golpe
de la aurora,
como un tambor, despierta,
gigantesco,
y se mueve.
Todas sus manos mueve,
su incesante organismo,
su dentadura extensa,
sus negocios
de sal, de sol, de plata,
todo
lo mueve, lo remueve
con sus arrasadores
manantiales,

and
afterward,
twilight.
Earth
binds to its face
the bituminous
mask.

But
the sea
takes no pleasure in sleep or repose;
does not die.
It grows big in the night;
its belly
is curved with the wet
of the stars like a bounty of wheat
in the sunrise, and grows big.
It quivers
and cries
like a child
astray in a dream
that only the shock
of the morning
awakens; it pounds on a drumskin
and gigantically
passes.
See: all its hands are alive,
its incessant anatomy,
the boundless unbaring of teeth;
its traffic
with silver and salt and the sun—
all
is shaken and turns on itself
in the leveling
fountainheads

con el combate
de su movimiento,
mientras
transcurre
el triste
otoño
de la tierra.

and the war of
mobility,
while slowly
the comfortless
autumn
of earth
comes to pass.

ODA A LA PANTERA NEGRA

Hace treinta y un años,
no lo olvido,
en Singapore, la lluvia
caliente como sangre
caía
sobre
antiguos muros blancos
carcomidos
por la humedad que en ellos
dejó besos leprosos.
La multitud oscura
relucía
de pronto en un relámpago
los dientes
o los ojos
y el sol de hierro arriba
como
lanza implacable.

Vagué por calles inundadas
betel, las nueces rojas
elevándose
sobre
camas de hojas fragantes,
y el fruto *Dorian*
pudriéndose en la siesta bochornosa.

De pronto estuve
frente a una mirada
desde una jaula
en medio de la calle
dos círculos
de frío,

BLACK PANTHERESS

Thirty-one years—
I haven't forgotten it:
In Singapore: a blood heat
of rain
on the mouldering white
of the walls
bitten
with wet
and the leprous kiss
of humidity:
the shadowy pack of the rain
that blazed suddenly back
and bared—in the lightning—
the teeth—
or the eyes—
the sun like implacable
iron,
a lance-point above me.

I loitered in alleyways drowning
in *betel,* red pods
aloft
on
the sweet-smelling leaf-bed;
the putrified fruit of the *Dorian*
in its sultry siesta.

And suddenly saw it:
the face in a cage
by my face,
midway in the street—
two circles
of cold,

dos imanes,
dos electricidades enemigas,
dos ojos
que entraron en los míos
clavándome
a la tierra
y a la pared leprosa.
Vi entonces
el cuerpo que ondulaba
y era
sombra de terciopelo,
elástica pureza,
noche pura.
Bajo la negra piel
espolvoreados
apenas la irisaban
no supe bien
si rombos de topacio
o hexágonos de oro
que se traslucían
cuando
la presencia
delgada
se movía.
La pantera
pensando
y palpitando
era
una
reina
salvaje
en un cajón
en medio
de la calle
miserable.

two magnets,
electric antagonists,
two eyeballs
that drilled into mine
and bolted me there
by the ground
and the leprous stockade.
Saw
the surge of her body
that shaded
to velvet,
the flexing perfection—
darkness made perfect,
Then, in the night of that skin
the tentative sparkle began
like a pollen-fall:
a rhombus of topaz
or the gold of a hexagon
—how could I name it?—
a flashing transparency
as
the tapering
presence
displaced itself:
the pantheress
throbbing and thinking
its thoughts,
a
barbarous
queen
in
a box
midway
on the trash
of the street.

De la selva perdida
del engaño.
del espacio robado,
del agridulce olor
a ser humano
y casas polvorientas
ella
sólo expresaba
con ojos
minerales
su desprecio, su ira
quemadora,
y eran sus ojos
dos
sellos
impenetrables
que cerraban
hasta la eternidad
una puerta salvaje.

Anduvo
como el fuego, y, como el humo,
cuando cerró los ojos
se hizo invisible, inabarcable noche.

Out of wilderness wasted
by perfidy,
the plunder of space
and the bittersweet reek of the living,
to whatever was human
in the powdery houses
only
the panther
of mineral eye
declared
her contempt, in the heat
of her rage.
Her eyes
were
unbreakable
seals
timelessly slammed
on the door
of a jungle.

She walked
like a holocaust; and closing her eyes,
she touched the invisible, boundless as smoke,
and was one with the night.

ODA A LA JARDINERA

Sí, yo sabía que tus manos eran
el alhelí florido, la azucena
de plata:
algo que ver tenías
con el suelo,
con el florecimiento de la tierra,
pero,
cuando
te vi cavar, cavar,
apartar piedrecitas
y manejar raíces
supe de pronto,
agricultora mía,
que
no sólo
tus manos
sino tu corazón
eran de tierra,
que allí
estabas
haciendo
cosas tuyas,
tocando
puertas
húmedas
por donde
circulan
las
semillas.

Así, pues,
de una a otra
planta

GIRL GARDENING

Yes: I knew that your hands were
a blossoming clove and the silvery
lily:
your notable way
with a furrow
and the flowering marl;
but
when
I saw you delve deeper, dig under
to uncouple the cobble
and limber the roots,
I knew in a moment,
little husbandman,
your heartbeats
were earthen
no less
than your hands;
that there,
you were
shaping
a thing that was always
your own,
touching
the drench
of those doorways
through
which
whirl
the seeds.

So,
plant after plant,
each

recién
plantada,
con el rostro
manchado
por un beso
del barro,
ibas
y regresabas
floreciendo,
ibas
y de tu mano
el tallo
de la alstromeria
elevó su elegancia solitaria,
el jazmín
aderezó
la niebla de tu frente
con estrellas de aroma y de rocío

Todo
de ti crecía
penetrando
en la tierra
y haciéndose
inmediata
luz verde,
follaje y poderío.
Tú le comunicabas
tus semillas,
amada mía,
jardinera roja:
tu mano
se tuteaba
con la tierra
y era instantáneo
el claro crecimiento.

fresh
from the planting,
your face
stained
with the kiss
of the ooze,
your flowering
went out
and returned,
you went out
and the tube
of the Alstroemeria
there under your hands
raised its lonely and delicate
presence, the jasmine
devised
a cloud for your temples
starry with scent and the dew.

The whole
of you prospered,
piercing down
into earth,
greening
the light
like a thunderclap
in a massing of leafage and power.
You confided
your seedlings,
my darling,
little red husbandman;
your hand
fondled
the earth
and straightway
the growing was luminous.

Amor, así también
tu mano
de agua,
tu corazón de tierra,
dieron
fertilidad
y fuerza a mis canciones.
Tocas
mi pecho
mientras duermo
y los árboles brotan
de mi sueño.
Despierto, abro los ojos,
y has plantado
dentro de mí
asombradas estrellas
que suben
con mi canto.

Es así, jardinera:
nuestro amor
es
terrestre:
tu boca es planta de la luz, corola,
mi corazón trabaja en las raíces.

Even so,
your watery
fingers,
the dust of your heart,
bring us word
of fecundity, love,
and summon the strength of my songs.
Touching
my heart
while I sleep
trees bloom
on my dream.
I waken and widen my eyes,
and you plant
in my flesh
the darkening stars
that rise
in my song.

So it is, little husbandman:
our loves
are
terrestrial:
your mouth is a planting of lights, a corolla,
and my heart works below in the roots.

ODA A LA LUZ MARINA

Otra vez, espaciosa
luz marina
cayendo de los cántaros
del cielo,
subiendo de la espuma,
de la arena,
luz agitada sobre
la extensión del océano,
como un
combate de cuchillos
y relámpagos,
luz de la sal caliente,
luz del cielo
elevado
como torre del mar sobre las aguas.

Dónde
están las tristezas?

El pecho se abre
convertido
en rama,
la luz sacude
en nuestro
corazón
sus amapolas,
brillan
en el día del mar
las cosas
puras
las piedras
visitadas
por la ola,

A LIGHT FROM THE SEA

Once more, the sea-light's
immensity,
the sky-fall
in flagons,
climbing the spume
and the sea-silt:
disturbance of light
in the ocean's extension,
thunderbolts,
a quarrel of knives,
lights
in the sweltering salts
and the sky,
upright
like a tower of brine on the waters.

Where
do the griefs go?

The breast opens out
like a branch
and its leafage;
light works
in our hearts
like a volley
of butterflies.
There shines
for the day of the sea
all the innocent
presences:
the pebble
embraced
by the wave,

los fragmentos
vencidos
de botellas,
vidrios
del agua,
suaves,
alisados
por sus dedos
de estrella.
Brillan
los
cuerpos
de los hombres salobres,
de las mujeres
verdes,
de los niños
como algas,
como
peces que saltan
en el cielo;
y cuando
una ventana
clausurada, un traje,
un monte oscuro,
se atreven
a competir
manchando la blancura,
llega la claridad a borbotones,
la luz
extiende sus mangueras
y ataca la insolente
sombra
con brazos blancos,
con manteles,
con talco y olas de oro,

the shipwrecked
debris
of the bottle glass,
glazes
of water,
suavities
honed by the touch
of a star.
There, burn
the
bodies:
bracken and salt
on the men,
the women
all green,
the children
like
pond-weeds,
fish-forms that leap
for the sky.
Should
a window's
recesses, the bulking of clothing,
a darkening lift of the land
presume
on that dazzle
or disfigure the brightness,
the clarities foam in the bubbles,
light
widens a sleeve
and harries the insolent
shadow
in a might of white arms,
altar cloths,
tinsel, in breakers of gold,

con estupenda espuma,
con carros de azucena.

Poderío
de la luz madurando en el espacio,
ola que nos traspasa
sin mojarnos, cadera
del universo,
                    rosa
renacedora, renacida;
abre
cada día tus pétalos,
tus párpados,
que la velocidad de tu pureza
extienda nuestros ojos
y nos enseñe a ver ola por ola
el mar
y flor a flor la tierra.

in marvels of spindrift
and tumbrils of lilies.

Light ripens its powers in the spaces.
O billow that pierces
without wetting the bather, pivot
and flank of a universe,
                              regenerate rose
re-arising:
open
each day with your petals
and eyelids,
grant us your cleanly celerities
to widen our onlooking;
bring us to see, in the end,
the sea moving, wave upon wave,
and flower after flower, all the earth.

ODA AL VIEJO POETA

Me dió la mano
como si un árbol viejo
alargara un gancho
sin
hojas y sin frutos.
Su
mano
que escribió desenlazando
los hilos y las hebras
del
destino
ahora estaba
minuciosamente
rayada
por los días, los meses y los años.
Seca en su rostro
era
la escritura
del tiempo,
diminuta
y errante
como
si allí estuvieran
dispucstos
las líneas y los signos
desde su nacimiento
y poco a poco
el aire
las hubiera erigido.

Largas líneas profundas,
capítulos cortados
por la edad en su cara,

POET GROWN OLD

He gave me his hand
like an old tree
that lengthens the fork
of its branches,
leafless
and fruitless.
His
hand
that unbound, while it wrote,
the fiber and weave
of
a destiny,
now rayed
with the hairline
striations:
the days and the months and the years.
Time
scribbled
its drouth
in his face,
wayward
and meager,
as if
to dispose
all the lines and the signs
of his birth,
until, little by little,
the air would erect what it saw
and establish it there.

Long lines where the depths were,
compendious chapters
for the years of his face,

Pablo Neruda / 265

signos interrogantes,
fábulas misteriosas,
asteriscos,
todo lo que olvidaron las sirenas
en la extendida
soledad de su alma,
lo que cayó del
estrellado cielo,
allí estaba en su rostro
dibujado.
Nunca el antiguo
bardo
recogió
con pluma y papel duro
el río derramado
de la vida
o el dios desconocido
que cortejó su verso,
y ahora,
en sus mejillas,
todo
el misterio
diseñó
con frío
el álgebra
de sus revelaciones
y las pequeñas,
invariables
cosas
menospreciadas
dejaron
en su frente
profundísimas
páginas
y

querulous symbols,
and equivocal fables,
asterisks—
whatever the sirens forgot
in an old
isolation of spirit,
or dropped
from the sky and the stars,
was scored
in his face.
Olden
and bardic,
his pen
never fixed
on the obdurate page
the river that spills
through our life
or the anonymous god
that attended his verses.
Now
on his cheekbones
the whole of
the mystery
charted
its algebra
in cold
revelations:
the little,
unvarying
slights
of the underprized,
cut hard
on the page of his
forehead;
and

hasta
en su
nariz
delgada,
como pico
de cormorán errante,
los viajes y las olas
depositaron
su letra
ultramarina.

Sólo
dos piedrecitas
intratables,
dos ágatas
marinas
en aquel
combate,
eran
sus ojos
y sólo a través de ellos
vi la apagada
hoguera,
una rosa
en las manos
del poeta.

Ahora
el traje
le quedaba grande
como si ya viviera
en una
casa
vacía,
y los huesos

starved
as the beak
of the wandering cormorant,
journeys and waters
had shored
on the dearth
of his
nose
their bluest
calligraphy.

Two chips
of intractable flint,
two watery
agates:
only that.
His eyes lived
embattled;
only there
could I summon
the blaze
in the cinder,
a rose
in the hands of
the poet.

Now
his clothing
outnumbered him,
he lived
in the void
of his clothes,
like a house.
All the bones

de todo
su cuerpo se acercaban
a la piel
levantándola
y era
de hueso,
de hueso que advertía
y enseñaba,
un pequeño
árbol, al fin, de hueso,
era el poeta
apagado
por la caligrafía
de la lluvia,
por los inagotables
manantiales del tiempo.

Allí le dejé andando
presuroso a su muerte
como
si lo esperara
también casi desnuda
en un parque sombrío
y de la mano
fueran
hasta
un desmantelado dormitorio
y en él durmieran
como dormiremos
todos
los hombres:
con
una rosa
seca
en

of his
body
drew close to
his skin
and faulted him upward:
a bone man
displayed, a bony
prefigurement,
a lessening tree
gone to bone, in the end,
a poet
put out
by the scrawl
of the rain
in the unquenchable
downpour of time.

I left him there,
nimble with dying,
walking toward death
as one who awaited a presence
stripped to the bone, like himself,
in a darkening park;
each by the other,
they moved
toward a
bedroom's dishevelment,
toward the sleep
we shall sleep out together,
whosoever
we are: a man
with
a withering
rose
in

una
mano
que también cae
convertida en polvo.

his
hand, dustily
fallen
to dust.

Navegaciones y Regresos / Voyages and Homecomings
(1959)

ODA A LAS COSAS ROTAS

Se van rompiendo cosas
en la casa
como empujadas por un invisible
quebrador voluntario:
no son las manos mías,
ni las tuyas,
no fueron las muchachas
de uña dura
y pasos de planeta:
no fue nada y nadie,
no fue el viento,
no fue el anaranjado mediodía,
ni la noche terrestre,
no fue ni la nariz ni el codo,
la creciente cadera,
el tobillo,
ni el aire:
se quebró el plato, se cayó la lámpara
se derrumbaron todos los floreros
uno por uno, aquel
en pleno octubre
colmado de escarlata,
fatigado por todas las violetas,
y otro vacío
rodó, rodó, rodó
por el invierno
hasta ser sólo harina
de florero,
recuerdo roto, polvo luminoso.

Y aquel reloj
cuyo sonido
era

THINGS BREAKING

Things fall apart
in our houses,
as if jarred by the whim
of invisible ravagers:
not your hand
or mine,
or the girls
with the adamant fingernails
and the stride of the planets:
there is nothing to point to, no one
to blame—not the wind
or the tawny meridian
or terrestrial darkness;
no one with a nose or an elbow
or the lengthening span of a hip,
or a gust of the wind
or an ankle:
yet the crockery smashes, the lamp tumbles over,
the flowerpots totter
one after another
crowning the lapsing October
with crimson,
wan with their surfeit of violets,
others holding their emptiness in, circling
and circling and circling
the winter,
till the bowl with its blossoms
is gruel,
a keepsake in ruins, a luminous dust.

And the clockface
whose cadences
uttered

la voz de nuestras vidas,
el secreto
hilo
de las semanas,
que una a una
ataba tantas horas
a la miel, al silencio,
a tantos nacimientos y trabajos,
aquel reloj también
cayó y vibraron
entre los vidrios rotos
sus delicadas vísceras azules,
su largo corazón
desenrollado.

La vida va moliendo
vidrios, gastando ropas,
haciendo añicos,
triturando
formas,
y lo que dura con el tiempo es como
isla o nave en el mar,
perecedero,
rodeado por los frágiles peligros,
por implacables aguas y amenazas.

Pongamos todo de una vez, relojes,
platos, copas talladas por el frío,
en un saco y llevemos
al mar nuestros tesoros:
que se derrumben nuestras posesiones
en un solo alarmante quebradero,
que suene como un río
lo que se quiebra
y que el mar reconstruya

our lifetimes,
the secretive
thread
of the weeks,
one after another,
yoking the hours
to the honey and quietude,
the travails and births without end—
even the clock
plunges downward, the delicate blues
of its viscera
pulse in the splintering glass
and its great heart
springs open.

Life grinds
on the glasses and powders, wearing us threadbare,
smashing to smithereens,
pounding
the forms;
whatever is left of its passing abides
like a ship or a reef in the ocean,
and perishes there
in the circle of breakable hazard
ringed by the pitiless menace of waters.

Let us gather them, once and for all—the clocks
and the platters, cups carven in cold—
into a poke with them all and
down to the sea with our treasure!
there let our furniture smash
in the sinister shock of a breaker;
let the things that are broken
call out like a river
and the sea render back to us whole

con su largo trabajo de mareas
tantas cosas inútiles
que nadie rompe
pero se rompieron.

in the might of its crosscurrents
all that we held of no worth,
the trumpery no hand has broken,
but still goes on breaking.

ODA AL PIANO

Estaba triste el piano
en el concierto,
olvidado en su frac sepulturero,
y luego abrió la boca,
su boca de ballena:
entró el pianista al piano
volando como un cuervo,
algo pasó como si cayera
una piedra
de plata
o una mano
a un estanque
escondido:
resbaló la dulzura
como la lluvia
sobre una campana,
cayó la luz al fondo
de una casa cerrada,
una esmeralda recorrió el abismo
y sonó el mar,
la noche,
las praderas,
la gota del rocío,
el altísimo trueno,
cantó la arquitectura de la rosa,
rodó el silencio al lecho de la aurora.

Así nació la música
del piano que moría,
subió la vestidura
de la náyade

PIANO

Midway in the concert,
the piano grew pensive,
ignored in its gravedigger's frock coat;
but later it opened its mouth
—the jaws of leviathan:
the pianist then entered his piano
and deployed like a crow;
something happened, like a silvery
downfall
of pebbles
or a hand
in a pond,
unobserved:
a trickle of sweetness
like rain
on the smooth of a bell,
light fell
through the padlocks and bolts of a house,
to the depths,
an emerald crossed the abysses,
the sea gave its sound
the night
and the dews
and the meadows,
the steepest ascents of the thunderbolt,
the symmetrical rose sang aloud
and quietness circled the milk of the morning.

So melody grew
in a dying piano,
the naiad's
investiture

del catafalco
y de su dentadura
hasta que en el olvido
cayó el piano, el pianista
y el concierto,
y todo fue sonido,
torrencial elemento,
sistema puro, claro campanario.

Entonces volvió el hombre
del árbol de la música.
Bajó volando como
cuervo perdido
o caballero loco:
cerró su boca de ballena el piano
y él anduvo hacia atrás,
hacia el silencio.

rose on the catafalque
from a margin of teeth,
piano, pianist,
and concerto plunged downward, oblivious,
till all was sonority,
torrential beginnings,
consummate gradation, a bell tower's clarities.

Then the man in the tree
of his music came back to us.
He came down like
a blundering crow on its course
or a lunatic dandy:
the whale-mouth closed up
and the man walked away
to a silence.

ODA AL GATO

Los animales fueron
imperfectos,
largos de cola, tristes
de cabeza.
Poco a poco se fueron
componiendo,
haciéndose paisaje,
adquiriendo lunares, gracia, vuelo.
El gato,
sólo el gato
apareció completo
y orgulloso:
nació completamente terminado,
camina solo y sabe lo que quiere.

El hombre quiere ser pescado y pájaro,
la serpiente quisiera tener alas,
el perro es un león desorientado,
el ingeniero quiere ser poeta,
la mosca estudia para golondrina,
el poeta trata de imitar la mosca,
pero el gato
quiere ser sólo gato
y todo gato es gato
desde bigote a cola,
desde presentimiento a rata viva,
desde la noche hasta sus ojos de oro.

No hay unidad
como él,
no tiene
la luna ni la flor
tal contextura:

CAT

The animal kingdom came
faultily:
too wide in the rump or too
sad-headed.
Little by little they disposed
their proportions,
invented their landscape,
collected their graces and satellites, and took to the air.
Only the cat
issued
wholly a cat,
intact and vainglorious:
he came forth a consummate identity,
knew what he wanted, and walked tall.

Men wish they were fishes or birds;
the worm would be winged,
the dog is a dispossessed lion;
engineers would be poets;
flies ponder the swallow's prerogative
and poets impersonate flies—
but the cat
intends nothing but cat:
he is cat
from his tail to his chin whiskers:
from his living presumption of mouse
and the darkness, to the gold of his irises.

His is that peerless
integrity,
neither moonlight nor petal
repeats
his contexture:

es una sola cosa
como el sol o el topacio,
y la elástica línea en su contorno
firme y sutil es como
la línea de la proa de una nave.
Sus ojos amarillos
dejaron una sola
ranura
para echar las monedas de la noche.

Oh pequeño
emperador sin orbe,
conquistador sin patria,
mínimo tigre de salón, nupcial
sultán del cielo
de las tejas eróticas,
el viento del amor
en la intemperie
reclamas
cuando pasas
y posas
cuatro pies delicados
en el suelo,
oliendo,
desconfiando
de todo lo terrestre,
porque todo
es inmundo
para el inmaculado pie del gato.

Oh fiera independiente
de la casa, arrogante
vestigio de la noche,
perezosa, gimnástico
y ajeno

he is all things in all,
like the sun or a topaz,
and the flexible line of his contour
is subtle and certain
as the cut of a bowsprit.
The gold of his pupils
leaves a singular
slash
and coins tumble out of the night.

Unorbed
little emperor,
landless conquistador,
minimal drawing-room tiger and conjugal
khan in a heaven
of aphrodisiacal rooftops:
you command
all the crosswinds of lust
in a hurricane,
you poise
your four delicate paws
on the ground
when you pass,
nosing the wind
and mistrusting
the universe,
as if
all were too gross
for a cat's incorruptible tread.

Wayward and proud
in the houses, a brazen
remainder of darkness,
torpid, gymnastic,
remote,

profundísimo gato,
policía secreta
de las habitaciones,
insignia
de un
desaparecido terciopelo,
seguramente no hay
enigma
en tu manera,
tal vez no eres misterio,
todo el mundo te sabe y perteneces
al habitante menos misterioso,
tal vez todos lo creen,
todos se creen dueños,
proprietarios, tíos
de gatos, compañeros,
colegas,
discípulos o amigos
de su gato.

Yo no.
Yo no suscribo.
Yo no conozco al gato.
Todo lo sé, la vida y su archipiélago,
el mar y la ciudad incalculable,
la botánica,
el gineceo con sus extravíos,
el por y el menos de la matemática,
los embudos volcánicos del mundo,
la cáscara irreal del cocodrilo,
la bondad ignorada del bombero,
el atavismo azul del sacerdote,
pero no puedo descifrar un gato.
Mi razón resbaló en su indiferencia,
sus ojos tienen números de oro.

an unfathomed profundity,
secret police
of the tenements,
and emblem
of vanishing velvets,
your kind
need not puzzle us, surely—
you, the least of
the mysteries
abroad in the world, known to us all, the pawn
of the lowliest householder—
or they think so!—
for each calls himself master,
proprietor, playfellow,
cat's uncle,
colleague,
the pupils of cats
or their cronies.

Not I:
I reckon things otherwise.
I shall never unriddle the cat.
I take note of the other things: life's archipelagoes,
the sea, the incalculable city,
botanical matters,
the pistil, the pistil's mutations,
plus-and-minus arithmetic,
volcanoes that funnel the earth
the improbable rind of the crocodile,
the fireman's unheeded benevolence,
the atavist blue of the clergyman—
but never the cat!
We do not concern him: our reasoning boggles,
and his eyes give their numbers in gold.

Espesa bestia pura,
San Elefante,
animal santo
del bosque sempiterno,
todo materia fuerte
fina
y equilibrada,
cuero
de
talabartería planetaria,
marfil
compacto, satinado,
sereno
como
la carne de la luna,
ojos mínimos
parar mirar, no para ser mirados,
y trompa
tocadora,
corneta
del contacto,
manguera
del
animal
gozoso
en
su
frescura,
máquina movediza,
teléfono del bosque,
y así
pasa tranquilo
y bamboleante

FROM: ELEPHANT

Gross innocent,
Saint Elephant,
blessed beast
of the perduring forests,
bulk of our palpable world
in its counterpoise,
mighty
and exquisite,
a saddlery's cosmos
in leather,
ivory
packed into satins
unmoved
like
the flesh of the moon,
minimal eyes
to observe, without being observed,
horn
virtuoso
and bugling
propinquity,
animal
waterspout
elate
in
its
cleanliness,
portable
engine
and telephone booth in a forest:
so
softly you go
in your swagger,

Pablo Neruda / 293

con su vieja envoltura,
con su ropaje
de árbol arrugado,
su pantalón
caído
y su colita.

No nos equivoquemos.
La dulce y grande bestia de la selva
no es el clown,
sino el padre
el padre en la luz verde,
es el antiguo
y puro
progenitor terrestre.

Total fecundación,
tantálica
codicia,
fornicación
y piel
mayoritaria,
costumbres
en la lluvia
rodearon
el reino
de los elefantes,
y fue
con sal
y sangre
la genérica guerra
en el silencio.

with your aging caparison
in the wrinkle and pile
of a tree's regimentals,
your pants
at your ankles,
trailing your tail-end.

Make no mistake:
that endeared and enormous
sojourner of jungles is nobody's clown;
he is patriarch,
father of emerald lights,
the ancient
and innocent
sire of the universe.

All the fruits of the earth,
and the longings
of Tantalus,
the multitudinous
skin
and the ways of
the rain
have encompassed
the kingdom of
elephants;
with brine
and
with blood
they accomplished the war
of their species in silence.

Las escamosas formas
el lagarto león,
el pez montaña,
el milodonto cíclope,
cayeron,
decayeron,
fueron fermento verde en el pantano,
tesoro
de las tórridas moscas
de escarabajos crueles.
Emergió el elefante
del miedo destronado.
Fue casi vegetal, oscura torre
del firmamento verde,
y de hojas dulces, miel
y agua de roca
se alimentó su estirpe . . .

The scale-bearing kind,
the lizards-turned-lion,
the fish in the mountains
and gargantuan ground sloth
succumbed
and decayed:
they
leavened the green of the bog,
a prize
for the sweltering fly
and the scarab's barbarity.
But the elephant rose
on the wreck of his fears—
almost a vegetable, a shadowy pylon
in his emerald heaven,
to suckle his young
on the sweet of the leaves, and the water
and honey of stones. . . .

Estravagario / Book of Vagaries
(1958)

LAS VIEJAS DEL OCÉANO

Al grave mar vienen las viejas
con anudados pañolones,
con frágiles pies quebradizos.

Se sientan solas en la orilla
sin cambiar de ojos ni de manos,
sin cambiar de nube o silencio.

El mar obsceno rompe y rasga,
desciende montes de trompetas,
sacude sus barbas de toro.

Las suaves señoras sentadas
como en un barco transparente
miran las olas terroristas.

Dónde irán y dónde estuvieron?
Vienen de todos los rincones,
vienen de nuestra propia vida.

Ahora tienen el océano,
el frío y ardiente vacío,
la soledad llena de llamas.

Vienen de todos los pasados,
de casas que fueron fragantes,
de crepúsculos quemados.

Miran o no miran el mar,
con el bastón escriben signos,
y borra el mar su caligrafía.

OLD WOMEN BY THE SEA

The old women come to the serious sea
with their withering shawls
and their fragile feet broken.

Alone on the beaches, they sit
without shifting their gaze or their hands
or the clouds or the quietness.

The ocean's obscenity shatters and slashes,
descends in a mountain of trumpets,
shakes a bullock's mustaches.

The matriarchs sit in their places, unmoved,
transparent, like ships on a sea,
observing the terrorist waves.

Where do they come from, where go to?
They move out of corners,
from the quick of our lives.

The ocean is theirs, now,
the vacancy, freezing and burning,
the solitude crowded with bonfires.

They move in the fullness of time
from the once-fragrant houses
and the char of the twilight.

They see and do not see the waters,
they write signs with their walking sticks,
and the sea blots their signatures.

Pablo Neruda / 301

Las viejas se van levantando
con sus frágiles pies de pájaro,
mientras las olas desbocadas
viajan desnudas en el viento.

Then the ancients move off
on frail bird's feet, upraised,
while a runaway surf
travels naked in the wind.

ESTACIÓN INMÓVIL

Quiero no saber ni soñar.
Quién puede enseñarme a no ser,
a vivir sin seguir viviendo?

Cómo continúa el agua?
Cuál es el cielo de las piedras?

Inmóvil, hasta que detengan
las migraciones su apogeo
y luego vuelen con sus flechas
hacia el archipiélago frío.

Inmóvil, con secreta vida
como una ciudad subterránea
para que resbalen los días
como gotas inabarcables:
nada se gasta ni se muere
hasta nuestra resurrección,
hasta regresar con los pasos
de la primavera enterrada,
de lo que yacía perdido,
inacabablemente inmóvil
y que ahora sube desde no ser
a ser una rama florida.

STATIONARY POINT

I would know nothing, dream nothing:
who will teach my non-being
how to be, without striving to be?

How can the water endure it?
What sky have the stones dreamed?

Immobile, until those migrations
delay at their apogee
and fly on their arrows
toward the cold archipelago.

Unmoved in its secretive life,
like an underground city,
so the days may glide down
like ungraspable dew:
nothing fails, or shall perish,
until we be born again,
until all that lay plundered
be restored with the tread
of the springtime we buried—
the unceasingly stilled, as it lifts
itself out of non-being, even now,
to be flowering bough.

PASTORAL

Voy copiando montañas, ríos, nubes,
saco mi pluma del bolsillo, anoto
un pájaro que sube
o una araña en su fábrica de seda,
no se me ocurre nada más: soy aire,
aire abierto, donde circula el trigo
y me conmueve un vuelo, la insegura
dirección de una hoja, el redondo
ojo de un pez inmóvil en el lago,
las estatuas que vuelan en las nubes,
las multiplicaciones de la lluvia.

No se me ocurre más que el transparente
estío, no canto más que el viento,
y así pasa la historia con su carro
recogiendo mortajas y medallas,
y pasa y yo no siento sino ríos,
me quedo solo con la primavera.

Pastor, pastor, no sabes
que te esperan?

Le sé, lo sé, pero aquí junto al agua,
mientras crepitan y arden las cigarras
aunque me esperen yo quiero esperarme,
yo también quiero verme,
quiero saber al fin cómo me siento,
y cuando llegue donde yo me espero,
voy a dormirme muerto de la risa.

PASTORAL

I go copying mountains and rivers and clouds:
I shake out my fountain pen, remark
on a bird flying upward
or a spider alive in his workshop of floss,
with no thought in my head; I am air,
I am limitless air where the wheat tosses,
and am moved by an impulse to fly, the uncertain
direction of leaves, the round
eye of the motionless fish in the cove,
statues that soar through the clouds,
the rain's multiplications.

I see only a summer's
transparency, I sing nothing but wind,
while history creaks on its carnival floats
hoarding medals and shrouds
and passes me by, and I stand by myself
in the spring, knowing nothing but rivers.

Shepherd-boy, shepherd-boy, don't you know
that they wait for you?

I know and I know it: but here by the water
in the crackle and flare of cicadas,
I must wait for myself, as they wait for me there:
I also would see myself coming
and know in the end how it feels to me
when I come to the place where I wait for my coming
and turn back to my sleep and die laughing.

Pablo Neruda / 307

V.

Sufro de aquel amigo que murió
y que era como yo buen carpintero.
Íbamos juntos por mesas y calles,
por guerras, por dolores y por piedras.
Cómo se le agrandaba la mirada
conmigo, era un fulgor aquel huesudo,
y su sonrisa me sirvió de pan,
nos dejamos de ver y V. se fué enterrando
hasta que lo obligaron a la tierra.

Desde entonces los mismos,
los que lo acorralaron mientras vivo
lo visten, lo sacuden,
lo condecoran, no lo dejan muerto,
y al pobre tan dormido
lo arman con sus espinas
y contra mí lo tiran, a matarme,
a ver quién mide más, mi pobre muerto
o yo, su hermano vivo.

Y ahora busco a quién contar las cosas
y no hay nadie que entienda estas miserias,
esta alimentación de la amargura:
hace falta uno grande,
y aquél ya no sonríe.
Ya se murió y no hallo a quién decirle
que no podrán, que no lograrán nada:
él, en el territorio de su muerte,
con sus obras cumplidas

V.

I mourn a dead friend,*
like myself, a good carpenter.
We traveled the streets and plateaus, among battles
and boulders and sorrows together.
How he widened his gaze
for my sake: a bag-of-bones blazing!
His smile was my bread
till we moved out of range and he hollowed a place in the
   ground
and they hounded him into it.

Since that time it is they,
those who hunted him down while alive
who adorn him and prod him
and pin him with ribbons and give him no peace;
they arm him with brambles—
poor slumberer!—
and hurl him against me, to kill me;
and who has the best of it, tell me: my poor, murdered
   friend,
or his brother who goes in my name?

This thing must be spoken: I look for a listener
but see no one to fathom that wretchedness,
that banquet of bitterness:
a greatness is gone
that will never smile more.
He is dead in the eons, and no one will hear me,
nothing will come of it, nothing avails us;
for he, in the shire of his death,
his anguish accomplished,

---

*The Peruvian poet (1892-1938), contemporary and friend of Neruda,
Cesár Vallejo. Died in exile, in Paris.

y yo con mis trabajos
somos sólo dos pobres carpinteros
con derecho al honor entre nosotros,
con derecho a la muerte a la vida.

and I with another employment,
are carpenters, poor carpenters only,
with a warrant of honor between us
and our titles to life and to death.

SONATA CON ALGUNOS PINOS

Al semisol de largos días
arrimemos los huesos cansados

olvidemos a los infieles
a los amigos sin piedad

el sol vacila entre los pinos
olvidemos a los que no saben

hay tierras dentro de la tierra
pequeñas patrias descuidadas

no recordemos a los felices
olvidemos sus dentaduras

que se duerman los delicados
en sus divanes extrapuros

hay que conocer ciertas piedras
llenas de rayos y secretos

amanecer con luz verde
con trenes desesperados

y tocar ese fin de mundo
que siempre viajó con nosotros

olvidemos al ofendido
que come una sola injusticia

los árboles dejan arriba
un semicielo entrecruzado

SONATA WITH SOME PINES

In the half-sun of the long days
let us bed our tired bones

and put out of mind the betrayers
the unpitying friends

the sun shakes in the pine trees
leave the heedless unheeded

there are kingdoms under the earth
little laggard republics

forget all the lucky ones
and abandon their tooth marks

let the finical sleep
on their sterile divans

while we pore on those curious stones
packed with lusters and riddles

and rise in the green light of dawn
with the desperate trains

let us finger the doomsday
that moved with us always

and forget how the injured ones
gnaw their injustice

above us the trees leave
a counter-crossed half-sky

Pablo Neruda / *313*

por alambres de pino y sombra
por el aire que se deshoja

olvidemos sin arrogancia
a los que no pueden querernos

a los que buscan fuego y caen
como nosotros al olvido

no hay nada mejor que las ocho
de la mañana en la espuma

se acerca un perro y huele el mar
no tiene confianza en el agua

mientras tanto llegan las olas
vestidas de blanco a la escuela

hay un sabor de sol salado
y sube en las algas mortuorias
olor a parto y pudridero

cuál es la razón de no ser?
a dónde te llevaron los otros?

es bueno cambiar de camisa
de piel de pelos de trabajo

conocer un poco la tierra
dar a tu mujer nuevos besos

pertenecer al aire puro
desdeñar las oligarquías

of pine wires and shadows
in disheveling air

let us put out of mind with no pride
those who never could cherish us

who hunted the holocaust
like ourselves and obliviously fell

nothing has greatness but sea-spray
at eight in the morning

a dog sniffs the sea-line and comes closer
mistrusting the water

the breakers drive landward
wearing white like a schoolboy

the sun tastes of salt
and the smell in the funeral seaweed
is of childbirth and charnel house

what does our nothingness seek?
and where will the others abandon you?

a changing of blouses and skins
and our hair and our callings: it is good

good to ponder the earth a little
kiss one's wife in the morning

to belong to the innocent air
and disdain oligarchies

cuando me fuí de bruma en bruma
navegando con mi sombrero

no encontré a nadie con caminos
todos estaban preocupados

todos iban a vender cosas
nadie me preguntó quién era

hasta que fuí reconociéndome
hasta que toqué una sonrisa

al semicielo y la enramada
acudamos con el cansancio

conversemos con las raíces
y con las olas descontentas

olvidemos la rapidez
los dientes de los eficaces

olvidemos la tenebrosa
miscelánea de los malignos

hagamos profesión terrestre
toquemos tierra con el alma.

when I journeyed from mist into mist
afloat in my hat

I met no one with highways
all went bemused

all had something to sell me
no one asked who I was

until one day I encountered myself
and was grazed by a smile

in the half-sky and the leafage
let us come with our tiredness

let us talk with the roots
and the malcontent waves

let us put out of mind all celerity
and the tooth of the capable

put the spleen from our minds
the malign miscellany

and make earthy our calling
and touch earth with our spirits.

SELECTED BIBLIOGRAPHY

1921   *La canción de la fiesta (Fiesta Song).* Santiago de Chile, Federación de Estudiantes de Chile.

1923   *Crepusculario (Twilight Book). Santiago de Chile,* Revista *Claridad* de la Federación de Estudiantes de Chile.

1924   *Veinte poemas de amor y una canción desesperada (Twenty Love Poems and A Desperate Song).* Santiago de Chile, Nascimento.

1925   *Tentativa del hombre infinito (Venture of Infinite Man).* Santiago de Chile, Nascimento.

       El habitante y su esperanza (Sojourner and his Hope). Prose. Santiago de Chile, Nascimento.

1926   *Anillos (Rings).* Prose. Santiago de Chile, Nascimento.

1933   *El hondero entusiasta (The Slinger-Enthusiast).* Santiago de Chile, Empresa Letras.

       Residencia en la tierra (Residence on Earth). Santiago de Chile, Nascimento.

1935   *Residencia en la tierra. I y II (1925–1935) (Residence on Earth).* In two volumes. Madrid, Cruz y Raya.

       Visiones de las hijas de Albión y El viajero mental, de William Blake (Visions of the Daughters of Albion and The Mental Traveler, by William Blake). Translation. Madrid, Cruz y Raya.

1937 *España en el corazón* (*Spain in the Heart*). Santiago de Chile, Ercilla.

1939 *Las furias y las penas* (*The Woes and the Furies*). Santiago de Chile, Nascimento.

1947 *Tercera residencia, 1935–1945* (*Residence on Earth*, III). Buenos Aires, Losada.

1950 *Canto general* (*General Song*). Mexico, D.F., Talleres Gráficos de la Nación.

1951 *Poesías completas* (*Complete Poems*). Buenos Aires, Losada.

1952 *Los versos del capitán* (*The Captain's Verses*). Buenos Aires, Losada.

   Las vidas del poeta. Memorias y recuerdos de Pablo Neruda (*Lives of the Poet. Memoirs and Recollections of Pablo Neruda*. Ten autobiographical chronicles in prose. "*O Cruzeiro Internacional*," Río de Janeiro, January 16 / June 10, 1962.

1954 *Las uvas y el viento* (*The Grapes and the Wind*). Santiago de Chile, Nascimento.

   Odas elementales (*Elemental Odes*). Buenos Aires, Losada.

1956 *Nuevas odas elementales* (*New Elemental Odes*). Buenos Aires, Losada.

1957 *Obras completas* (*Complete Works*). Buenos Aires, Losada.

Tercer libro de las odas (*Third Book of Odes*). Buenos Aires, Losada.

1958   *Estravagario* (*Book of Vagaries*). Buenos Aires, Losada.

1959   *Navegaciones y regresos* (*Voyages and Home-comings*). Buenos Aires, Losada.

1961   *Cien sonetos de amor* (*One Hundred Love Sonnets*). Buenos Aires, Losada.

Las piedras de Chile (*The Stones of Chile*). Buenos Aires, Losada.

Cantos ceremoniales (*Ceremonial Songs*). Buenos Aires, Losada.

1962   *Plenos poderes* (*Full Powers*). Buenos Aires, Losada.

1964   *Memorial de Isla Negra* (*Black Island Memorial*). Five volumes entitled: I, *Donde nace la lluvia* (*Where the Rains Begin*); II, *La luna en el laberinto* (*Moon in the Labyrinth*); III, *El cruel fuego* (*The Cruel Fire*); IV, *El cazador de raices* (*The Root Hunter*); V, *Sonata crítica* (*Critical Sonata*). Buenos Aires, Losada.

1968   *La barcarola* (*Barcarole*). Buenos Aires, Losada.